LEECH LAKE
Yesterday and Today

by
Duane R. Lund
Ph.D.

Distributed by
Adventure Publications, Inc.
P.O. Box 269
Cambridge, MN 55008

ISBN 1-885061-53-6

LEECH LAKE
Yesterday and Today

First Printing, 1998

Printed in the United States of America
by
Nordell Graphic Communications, Inc.
Staples, Minnesota 56479

TABLE OF CONTENTS

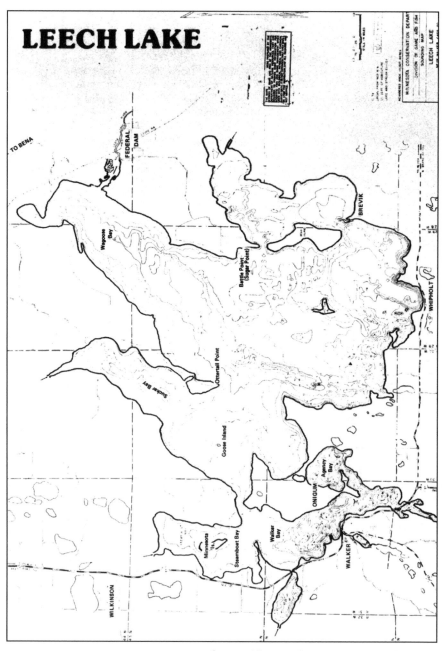

Courtesy Minnesota Department of Natural Resources

CHAPTER I

The Lake in
Prehistoric Times

Leech Lake

- third largest body of water entirely within Minnesota; only the Red Lakes have more wilderness shoreline (Lower Red Lake and Mille Lacs are larger)
- home of the Pillager band of Ojibwe, the Dakota Sioux and all unknown number of tribes before them
- scene of historic conflicts between Native American tribes
- important fur trade center
- setting for the last military–Indian war in the United States
- location of one of the largest pine tree logging operations in history
- today, its tourism drives the economy of North Central Minnesota

What a history! What a lake!

The size and shape of the Leech Lake we know today was created by the completion of a dam in 1884[1] at its northeast corner at the Leech Lake River outlet. The dam raised the water level nearly seven feet. We can define the lake prior to that time by eliminating all water less than seven feet deep. Needless to say, prehistoric Leech Lake was considerably smaller than the lake we enjoy today. The dam was constructed to create a reservoir which would help control the water levels of the Mississippi River—more water when it was needed to float logs; less water when flood control was a concern.

In 1909, the U.S. Corps of Engineers designed a plan to connect Leech Lake and Lake Winnibigoshish by digging a canal. Congress even appropriated the money, but it was never constructed. Although "Winnie" has less shoreline than Leech, it contains more cubic feet of water. By con-

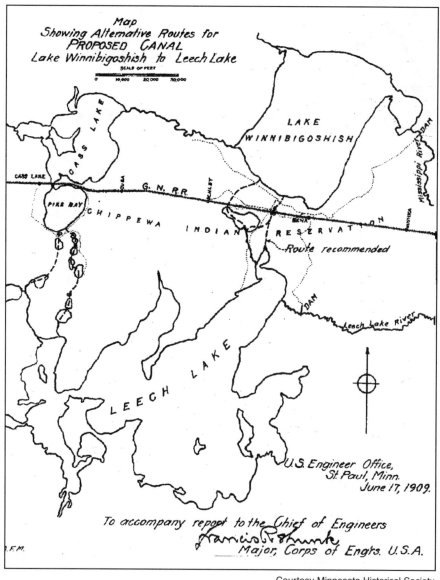

Map
Showing Alternative Routes for
PROPOSED CANAL
Lake Winnibigoshish to Leech Lake

The canal that never was.

necting the two lakes it was thought there would be improved control of water levels on the Mississippi. "Winnie" does have its own dam (on the Mississippi outlet); it was constructed between 1880 and 1882. Apparently the Corps of Engineers decided the canal would not make enough difference to justify the cost.

Geologists tell us that the approximate size and shape of Leech Lake prior to the construction of its dam was pretty well established by 2000 B.C. Many of the Indian village sites prior to the building of the dam are now at least partially under water.

Going back further, prehistoric Lake Agassiz covered most of what is now northwestern Minnesota and portions of the Dakotas, Manitoba and Ontario. It was larger than all of the Great Lakes combined and contained what is now the Red River Valley, the Red Lakes, Lake of the Woods, Lake Winnipeg and Lake Manitoba. Leech Lake was not included in that huge inland sea, but it was close by and that did have an impact.

Lake Agassiz was created by the meltdown of the last glacier, eight to twelve thousand years ago. (There were probably seven glaciers in all.)

It is truly hard to believe that the Leech Lake area was once covered by glaciers more than one mile thick! There was probably no visible life of any kind on or under the compacted ice and snow. The geography was carved out as the last glacier, called the Pleistocene, moved, grinding boulder against boulder—gouging out the hills and valleys of the landscape.[2] Towards the end, the meltdown was quite rapid and the huge volume of water not only filled the low spots, forming lakes, but also spawned torrential rivers which carved deep channels. The impressive gorges found along the Minnesota and Mississippi Rivers (below where it is joined by the Minnesota) were formed by the gigantic Glacial River Warren.[3]

The drying-up of the huge lake was apparently in stages because ridges which mark the beaches of the receding lake may be seen today from the air or even from some of the highways in the region. Archeologists have discovered village sites on these beaches which would indicate that the earliest people followed the lake north as it dried up.

We know that the first humans to live in the area were contemporary with the animal life of the Ice Age. Ancient burial mounds have been explored which contained ornaments, pottery, tools and weapons made of stone and bone. Some of these artifacts were made of live ivory[4] from the enormous tusks of the woolly mammoth. Since these people were the first inhabitants, at least they did not have to conquer some other tribe in order to move in. They no doubt, however, had their hands full just managing to survive in the hostile environment.

The animal and bird life was very different from today. Not only did the woolly mammoth roam the area but there were varieties of deer (the stag-moose), beaver and bison far larger than the animals we now know. In fact, there were differences even as recently as the coming of the French to this part of North America in the 1600's. Caribou were common then and there were more moose, elk and bear than deer. Passenger pigeons were so numerous it was said that migrating flocks darkened the sky. Today they are extinct.

If archeologists are correct in their conclusion that the last of the glaciers receded between eight and ten thousand years ago, then we can conclude that humans have been in this area a very long time indeed. Perhaps we can better comprehend just how long if we understand that Europeans have been here less than five percent of that human history. Even the Dakota Sioux, the first tribe to come into the area that is still in Minnesota, did not arrive until about 1000 A.D., which represents only about 10 percent of human occupation. Compared to the Dakota Sioux, the Ojibwe were really "Johnnies-come-lately," arriving in the 1600's along with the whites. The Ojibwe pushed the Dakota Sioux out of the woodlands of what is now Minnesota and Wisconsin by 1739.

To give us a better sense of the lake's history, it may help to remember that the beginning of this historic Ojibwe–Dakota Sioux conflict occurred before the American Revolution.

So where did the first inhabitants of this area come from anyway? Archeologists believe they were descendants of migrants from Asia who had originally crossed to North America by way of the Bering Straits[6] to Alaska. It is thought they then moved down the west coast. From there they migrated east across the continent. One has to wonder why they would leave the pleasant and relatively mild climate of what is now Washington, Oregon and California to travel east over a mountain range, across deep rivers, and through a hostile wilderness just to chase a glacier north into the land of woolly mammoths, short face bears and saber-toothed tigers! Were they just curious and wanting to explore? Was there a food shortage? Were they looking for an easier way of life? Or had the west coast become crowded enough so that they decided to find a safer place free from the dangers of attack? The author's guess is "all of the above" with the latter perhaps being the most important reason. Food may have been a problem. We know from oral histories that as recently as a few hundred years ago some tribes became nomadic because of food shortages caused by droughts or because animals upon which they were dependent for food and clothing were becoming scarce. In the 1700's the French recorded times along the present Minnesota–Ontario border when big game and fur bearers died off from disease and/or over-hunting and became critically scarce. So it is possible the tribes moved because of a shortage of food.

It is believed that these earliest Native Americans came from a variety of places in Asia[7] because of significant differences among the tribes. Their languages are different; even the root words of tribes that have been in contact for hundreds of years are different. There are also differences in physical appearance. The Dakota Sioux, for example, are relatively tall, while the Ojibwe are of a stockier build. There are also differences in culture including religion, food, pottery, implements, games, etc.

Yet, in spite of these differences, these first peoples had much in common and, indeed, much in common with us. After all, they were human beings, and like us they surely worked for a living, built shelters, clothed themselves according to current styles, played games, developed friendships, laughed, loved, fought, cried, worshipped and cared for their children. They probably lived as families and had special ties with the clans to whom they were related.

We will never know how long the very first inhabitants lived in peace or whether some disease claimed them before some other tribe destroyed them, pushed them out, or assimilated them. Surely North America was relatively sparsely populated in those first thousands of years and there should have been room for all. Yet, human nature, being what it is, there were no doubt conflicts. "The grass was always greener" elsewhere then, just as it is today and one tribe would no doubt covet another's territory. In the case of America's heartland there was a lot to covet. The area had both prairie and woodlands where all kinds of animals and birds could be found. Of course, that assumes similarity to the flora and fauna of recorded time. The lakes and streams were probably full of fish.

We do know there was considerable conflict in prehistoric times because large numbers of projectile heads have been found in areas where neither oral nor recorded history tells of battles.

The islands of Leech Lake are good places to find projectile heads, particularly just after ice-out or after a heavy rain. We know from oral history that islands were the last homes of the Dakota Sioux and the first homes of the conquering Ojibwe in the 1700s (because they were easier to defend) and so they were the scenes of much fighting and therefore some of these arrowheads were possibly from those battles. Because the tribes did not have muzzleloaders at that time, it is likely that many of these artifacts are prehistoric. Surely spears were not effective weapons against bows and guns in 18th century battles, and yet spearheads are occasionally found.[7]

It is not surprising that the farther back in time we go the more difficult it is to find artifacts of those earliest cultures. We do have, however, considerable information about a tribe of people who probably entered our woodlands about the time of Christ. They settled along the Boundary Waters, between Minnesota and Canada and buried their dead in enormous mounds. They are called "the Laurel Culture" and some of the largest mounds are located near Laurel, Minnesota.

The Laurel people may have come from the Pacific Coast or the Gulf of Mexico because shell ornaments have been found in their burial mounds which are of that origin. Their mounds are the largest found in this part of the continent; some are as high as forty feet and over 100 feet in length. There is evidence that these mounds contain the remains of several generations, indicating that these people lived here for quite some time. Other artifacts found in the mounds include sheet copper (probably mined on Lake Superior), decorated pieces of pottery, harpoons, and a variety of projectile heads. The abundance of arrowheads has left archeologists to speculate that these people may have introduced the bow and arrow to this region. It is also of interest that the bones were buried in bundles, indicating that the bodies were probably placed in trees or on scaffolds and allowed to decompose before burial. The marrow had been removed from some of the larger bones and the brains removed from some of the skulls shortly after death. In some cases the eye sockets had been filled with clay. Some archeologists have concluded there may have been certain cannibalistic rituals following death. The Laurel people were about the same height as we are today. That is surprising in that we know the human race has grown taller over the years. Soldiers in World War II were taller on the average than their fathers who fought in World War I. Suits of armor worn by knights in Medieval times would indicate that men were shorter in that day. Interesting that these peoples who lived 2,000 years ago were our size.

Although there is no evidence of these huge mounds in the Leech Lake region, artifacts have been found that may indicate the Laurel peoples moved through this area on their way north and could have lived here for a time. An early white resident reported finding a large mound (bigger than a beaver house) with bones in it on the shore at the mouth of the Sucker River.

Some archeologists believe that the earliest mound builders on this part of the continent were the Hopewell Indians of what is now southern Minnesota. Other prehistoric cultures built effigy mounds shaped like animals or birds. White settlers found many of these in Minnesota when they arrived but they have long since fallen victim to the plow.

Sometime around 1000 A.D. a new people arrived in what is now northern Minnesota and Wisconsin and established what has been called the "Blackduck Culture". Whether they pushed the Laurel people out or assimilated them is not known, possibly some of each. The Blackduck people buried their dead in pits and then built mounds over the remains. There are literally hundreds of these mounds in the Leech Lake region, and there are a considerable number along the shoreline of Leech Lake itself. Bear island and Mounds Point are examples. The Blackduck Culture prevailed in the woodlands until the 1600s when those tribes were pushed out by the Dakota Sioux. This was the first conflict between Native American tribes in this area that we can fairly accurately date.

The Blackduck Culture may have included several tribes, some of which are known today but now live in Manitoba or Ontario.

Oral history tells us that the Assiniboine were chased by their Sioux cousins, the Winnebagos, out of southern Wisconsin. It is thought the Assiniboine originally arrived in Wisconsin from the south or southwest. The Assiniboine probably were in Minnesota for a time before settling in Ontario and Manitoba. The Dakota Sioux, allthough related to the Assiniboine did not let them stay in what is now Minnesota, but pushed them farther north. It is no wonder the Assiniboine later joined the Cree and the Ojibwe in driving the Dakotas out of the woodlands.

According to oral history of the Gros Ventre and the Mandans[8] (they lived along the Missouri River in North Dakota), their forefathers previously lived in what is now Minnesota. The Gros Ventre once showed Ojibwe visitors a map drawn on birchbark which indicated they had once resided on Sandy Lake. Two Canadian Algonquin tribes, the Cree and the Ottawa, lived in northern Minnesota before the Dakota Sioux invasion. The Monsonis (Algonquin-related) were also in the border country during this period. It is not surprising that many of the artifacts that have been found in this region are from the Blackduck Culture. It is believed, for example, that the paintings still visible on the rock cliffs of the Boundary Waters and the Lake of the Woods were the works of the Blackduck Indians.

The Mandans are a particularly interesting people in that they were light complected and some had blond or red hair and blue eyes. Other tribes and early white visitors, such as the La Verendryes (a family of French–Canadian explorers), concluded they were of European origin or at least had assimilated whites. They even lived in walled villages, some with moats. The houses were arranged as though on streets. According to oral history, they also were Minnesotans for a time and may have been in the central lakes area. Although the Kensington Runestone, which tells the story of Vikings in the Alexandria area (found in the year 1898), has not been accepted as valid by some historians, it is a remarkable coincidence, if nothing else, that this tribe with European blood at one time probably lived in or near that area.

Leech Lake artifacts left behind by the Blackduck Culture include pots and a great abundance of pot fragments. Most of the woodland tribes had elongated pots, in contrast to the rounder pots of the prairie Indians, such as the Dakota Sioux. Remnants of both kinds of pots have been found around Leech Lake. One tribe that live on Rice Point on the west side of Sucker Bay decorated the inside of the lip of the pot, possibly to bless the foods or liquids as they were poured from the container. This is also a characteristic of a prehistoric tribe of present-day Illinois. They may have been the same people.

Although hard evidence is fragmentary, it is possible, and even likely, that all of these tribes we have mentioned visited Leech Lake and may have called it "home" for a time.

As we look at Leech Lake even today, it is easy to understand why so many Native American tribes chose to live here, and why they were willing to shed blood to capture and to keep it. The lake's many rice beds provided a grain that could be stored for year-around use. Fur bearing animals were in abundance, providing food, clothing and shelter. Birch, cedar and spruce trees were plentiful and provided materials for building canoes[9]. The waters of the lake had an abundance of fish. Early explorers and traders described the whitefish as "comparable to those found in Lake Superior" and Muskies and Northern Pike as "three and four feet long." Leech is connected by the Leech Lake River to the Mississippi River, and thereby to many other lakes, both north and south, making travel by water possible for thousands of miles. Leech Lake was a paradise then, and for those of us today who have a love affair with this beautiful body of water, it remains a paradise.

This first chapter has dealt with the beginnings of Leech Lake and its prehistoric history. Let us close with a beautiful Native American legend of its origin.

More moons back than any Chippewa can remember, when all the Indian tribes were away except a woman and her daughter, an evil spirit one day captured the maiden and carried her away to a great dry plain where he lived in a wigwam of solid rock. While pining for freedom she was visited by an emissary of the supreme deity of the Indians, who gave her a peculiar black stone and told her to make of it a spear and strike with it a certain spot on the rocks. She did as the spirit told her and at once a great spring of water welled out and flowed rapidly over the plain. It began to fill all the vast space, and as it rose, the maiden climbed higher and higher until she almost reached the top of the rock, when the water ceased rising. Meanwhile the evil spirit was surrounded by the water and was compelled to remain in the cave of rocks for all time and his moanings are heard ever above the soft winds which at all times prevail over Ga-sa-qua-ji-mai-gog-sa-ai-gan, now known as Leech Lake! This is how Leech Lake was formed. The Indian maiden escaped in a frail birch canoe that came floating from the shore one day. The land on which she climbed is pointed out as Bear Island.[10]

[1]Construction began in 1882.

[2]For further information about the rather complex and unique terrain left by the glaciers in this area, consult "Glaciers and Glacial Geology of the Leech Lake Watershed," by Robert C. Melchior and John O. Annexstad. 1996.

[3]For further information, consult "The Historic Upper Mississippi" by this author.

[4]Ivory from the tusks of animals recently killed.

[5]The land masses of North America and Asia are believed to have been joined together at one time.

[6]A small minority of historians speculate that a single tribe may have crossed over from Asia and that the language and other cultural differences came from separation and the passage of thousands of years of time. Others believe the various groups came from as far away as the Mideast and may be some of the lost tribes of Israel. Recent findings indicate at least two major migrations from different origins in Asia.

[7]French explorers did report a few spears in use by Native Americans in that day, however.

[8]For more information about the Mandans, consult "The Lake of the Woods, Vol.II, Earliest Accounts," by this author.

[9]Birchbark served as the skin; the struts were made from cedar and spruce, and gum was used to seal the cracks.

[10]Brochure, Walker Chamber of Commerce, 1972.

CHAPTER II

The Dakota Sioux and Then the Ojibwe Call Leech Lake Home

The Dakota Sioux took control of Leech Lake sometime in the early 1600's. To learn anything about inhabitants of the lake prior to that time, we have to depend upon the skills of the archeologists as they interpret the artifacts found here. They tell us that the Blackduck Indians controlled the woodlands of northern Minnesota, including Leech Lake, for several centuries before the coming of the Sioux. It is their best guess that the Blackduck culture was probably dominant from about 1000 A.D. to the coming of the Dakota Sioux to the Minnesota woodlands in the 1600's. The Dakota Sioux were a family of tribes within the Sioux Nation.

THE SIOUX NATION

Dakota, Lakota or Nakota[1] (with seven councils)
   Sisseton
   Teton
   Yankton
   Yanktonai
   Wahpeton
   Wahpakute
   Mdewakanton
Iowa
Oto
Missouri
Omaha
Osage
Ponca
Hidatsa
Crow
Mandan
Assiniboine
Winnebago

During the time period that the Blackducks were in the northern wood-lands of what is now called Minnesota (1000 A.D. to the 1600's), various Sioux tribes occupied the prairies of the western portion of what we now call the Midwest—including the prairies of western and southern Minnesota. Because the Sioux made such extensive use of the Mississippi and its tributaries, they are sometimes referred to as the "Mississippi Culture." Artifacts lead archeologists to believe that the Dakota Sioux entered the Minnesota prairies about the same time (1000 A.D.) as the Blackduck Indians moved into the northern woodlands. The timing may have been coincidental, or, it is possible the Sioux forced the Blackduck snorth. After all, we know it was the Dakota Sioux who invaded the wood-lands in the 1600's and pushed the Blackducks north into what we now call the "Boundary Waters" and southern Canada.

The stay of the Dakota Sioux in the northern woodlands including Leech Lake was relatively brief — probably a little more than 100 years. In 1739, the Ojibwe and their allies, the Cree and Assiniboin in particu-lar, forced the Sioux back south and west onto the prairies.

The Ojibwe, as we have already mentioned, are relative newcomers to this part of the continent. They are a member of the Algonquin Nation.

THE ALGONQUIN NATION
Ojibwe (also called Chippewa or Anishinaubay)[2]
Ottawa
Sac
Fox
Potawatomi
Illinois
Shawnee
Miami
Kickapoo
Menominee
Cree

In 1600, the Algonquin tribes occupied the eastern portion of the Midwest, with the Ojibwe as far east as New England. They were neigh-bors of the hostile Iroquois family of tribes. Because of the impact the Iroquois had on the Ojibwe, we will list them as well.

THE IROQUOIS NATION

Mohawk	Tuscarora
Oneida	Erie
Onondaga	Hurons
Cayuga	
Seneca	
(these five had a close alliance)	

The Iroquois were among the first to acquire guns from the early white colonists and with this tremendous advantage drove the Ojibwe west on both sides (north and south) of the Great Lakes. Some sources claim that upwards of 10,000 Ojibwe were killed in the process. During the 1600's, the Ojibwe came far enough west to occupy what is now Wisconsin and an area north of Lake Superior, thus becoming neighbors to the Dakota Sioux.

As white explorers, accompanied by their priests, ventured westward they found the Ojibwe scattered over a large area, both north and south of Lake Superior. When missionaries arrived at Sault Ste. Marie in 1640, they found a sizable concentration of Ojibwe. This village grew to an estimated population of 2000 by 1680–a virtual metropolis by the standards of the northern tribes. After 1680 the Ojibwe moved farther west and the village declined in both size and importance. A new concentration developed at La Point[3] – on Madeline Island at the mouth of Chequamegon Bay on Lake Superior. This new capital of the Ojibwe Nation eventually had a population of about 1,000.

The Ojibwe migration routes led both north and south of Lake Superior; the majority chose the southern route and settled in Wisconsin. Those using the northern way settled along the north shore of Lake Superior and around Rainy Lake and Lake of the Woods. Contrary to what we might expect, there was little confrontation at first between the Ojibwe and the Sioux. The basic reason was economic. The French needed the furs of the Minnesota Lake region and knew virtually none would be available if the Sioux and Ojibwe were at war. The Sioux and the Ojibwe realized too that there would be no trade items available to them if they had to spend their time defending themselves against an enemy instead of collecting furs. Du Luth was the chief negotiator and genuine hero of the peace-keeping effort. He wintered with the Ojibwe at Sault Ste. Marie in 1678-79 and during that time developed a good working relationship with both the French traders and the Indians. With the coming of the ice break-up in the spring, Du Luth led a band of Ojibwe to a site near the city which now bears his name, and there held a council with several tribes in an attempt to expand the fur trade industry into Minnesota and southern Ontario. At this meeting, representatives of the Dakota, Cree, and Assiniboin pledged friendship and cooperation with the French and Ojibwe. No mean accomplishment. Because there were so few French traders, the Ojibwe were to serve as middlemen, representing the French in trading with the Sioux and other tribes. It worked for about 60 years. Du Luth also used the occasion to lay claim to the entire upper Mississippi area for France. In the same year (1679) Du Luth founded a trading post at Grand Portage on Lake Superior. From this base he established trade with the Sioux tribes of the lake region with the Ojibwe as the traders. Grand Portage was destined to become the rendezvous point for the voyageurs from Montreal ("porkeaters") and those from Lake Athabasca and other western points ("men of the north"). Because it was impossible to travel all the way from Montreal to the trading posts in the west and return in a single season, a meeting place was necessary for the exchange of furs and trade goods. Grand Portage was that place. This rendezvous, in July of each year, was an occasion for great celebration.

Trade developed rapidly. LaSalle reported in 1682 that the Ojibwe were trading with the Dakotas as far as 150 miles to the west. The peaceful arrangement allowed large numbers of Ojibwe to settle in Wisconsin and along both the north and south shores of Lake Superior. But the peace was too good to last. The Sioux of the prairies (Lakota and Nakota) had not been included in Du Luth's conference and they frequently sent raiding parties into the Boundary Waters. By 1730 the truce was an uneasy one.

It was this testy atmosphere that greeted the French–Canadian explorer, Pierre La Verendrye, upon his arrival at Lake of the Woods in 1732. His construction of Fort St. Charles on the Northwest Angle of that lake helped keep the peace for a time, but the warpath which led from the plains of the Dakota to its terminal point at present day Warroad, on Lake of the Woods, was once again in use. La Verendrye, like other Frenchmen, allied himself with the Ojibwe, Cree and Assiniboine. It is not surprising, therefore, that the Sioux eventually launched a direct attack on the French. The Nakota[4] massacre on Lake of the Woods of twenty-one Frenchmen – including La Verendrye's eldest son, Jean Baptiste, and his priest, Father Alneau – really marked the beginning of all-out war between the Dakotas and the Ojibwe and their friends the Crees and the Assiniboines. In the same year (1736) the Ojibwe gained a measure of revenge for La Verendrye by launching a raiding party from La Pointe into southeastern Minnesota. The Cree, Assiniboine and some Ojibwe had begged La Verendrye to lead an attack against the Sioux, but in his wisdom he refused. He knew that open warfare would bring more Sioux to that area and could very well mean the end for some time to the fur trade business. His entire expedition was financed by Montreal merchants who had been growing more and more demanding for a better return on their investment. Without furs there would be no support from the East.

La Verendrye reminded the Cree, Assiniboine, Monsonis and the Ojibwe that it was the Nakota Sioux from the Dakota prairies, not the Dakota Sioux of the woodlands, who killed his men. He addressed the Ojibwe in particular, pointing out the good relations they had developed with the Dakota Sioux as they brought them trading goods in exchange for furs. La Verendrye made it clear to all tribes that the French had no quarrel with the Sioux of the woodlands. His efforts were in vain as raiding parties were sent against the Sioux from what is now Canada and western

Wisconsin. Within three short years after the Lake of the Woods massacre, the Dakota Sioux were dislodged from all of their Minnesota woodlands strongholds, including Leech Lake.

The first attacks on Leech were not by the Ojibwe, but by their allies the Crees and Assiniboines from the north. Launching their attack from their Lake of the Woods and boundary water villages, they drove down on the Red Lakes, Winnibigoshish, Cass and then Leech. The Ojibwe seemed almost reluctant at first to join battle. Perhaps it was because their leadership still felt a loyalty to the French and their pursuit of peace among the tribes. However, when they had once committed themselves, it was with a vengeance. The Dakota villages at Sandy Lake were among the first to fall to the Ojibwe and their allies — and this site was to become the new capital of the Ojibwe Nation. Located on the watershed between Lake Superior and the Mississippi lake region at the end of the Savanna portage, it was the key to control of the entire area. The Cree were the first to establish villages on Leech Lake following the rout of the Sioux.

Thus, by 1739, the Dakotas had fled from their lake area strongholds and had moved their families to the prairies, and back into the southern part of the state — particularly along the Minnesota River. The once powerful Mille Lacs village of Kathio—what was left of it—was moved to the mouth of the Rum River. But the war was by no means over. It was really the beginning of a hundred year's war. No sooner would the Sioux be driven from an area than they would plan a counterattack. If the Ojibwe or their allies moved out of an area, the Dakotas moved back in. Sometimes old village sites were even resettled by the original Sioux families. Although the Dakotas had been driven from their strongholds, they certainly had not given up; nor were the Ojibwe and their allies strong enough to occupy and control the area. When villages were first established by the Ojibwe and their allies, they were often wiped out — women, children and all. All of northern Minnesota soon became a virtual no man's land inhabited mostly by marauding war parties. The bands were not large — usually less than 100 braves in number. From 1739 to 1766, few tried to "live" in the area, and all who entered did so with intent to wage war. But when the ice went out of the lakes in the spring of 1766, the Ojibwe organized an army of about 400 warriors from their villages along Lake Superior and throughout Wisconsin. When the war party left Fond du Lac it was said that a man standing on a high hill could not see the end or the beginning of the line formed by the Indians walking in single file — as was their custom.

By mid-May, the better-armed Ojibwe had met and soundly defeated a much larger army of Dakotas, perhaps as many as 600 braves. The Dakotas at first fell back to Leech Lake and solidified their forces. Their first strategy was to occupy the islands of the lake. If they had been content to wait it out here until reinforcements arrived, they would have been relatively safe and could have held out for some time. However, over eager and confident, the Dakotas made a grave error in strategy. They divided their forces and launched three simultaneous attacks on Pembina, Rainy Lake and Sandy Lake. They lost on all three fronts and the resultant disaster was the turning point of the war. The Sioux fell back to their villages west of the Mississippi and along the Minnesota River and they were able to keep their stronghold on the Mississippi at the mouth of the Rum River.

The Ojibwe were for the first time truly in control of the lake region and a serious effort was made to settle the area. Sandy Lake continued as the headquarters for their operations but villages soon appeared on the Red Lakes, Winnibigoshish, Cass Lake, Leech Lake and Mille Lacs. Just as the islands of Leech Lake had been the last strongholds of the Dakotas they became the first homes of the Cree and Ojibwe in the area. For even though the Ojibwe had effectively defeated the Dakotas, Sioux war parties would return again and again for many years to view their old village sites, visit the burial places of their ancestors, and administer vengeance to the Ojibwe. In fact, if the Ojibwe villages had not been replenished continuously with settlers from the east, they surely would have been annihilated.

We shall see in the next chapter how the fighting continued, with few interruptions, for more than 100 years — up to the time of the Civil War (1862).

Because the Dakota Sioux and the Ojibwe have played such important roles in the history of Leech Lake, it is appropriate that before going on we take a closer look at the two cultures.

First, let us generalize that the people of these two great tribes were far more alike than they were different. Both, while in Minnesota, were dependent upon the woods, lakes, prairies, and streams for survival. The trees, especially the birch, furnished materials for both shelter and transportation. Animal life provided meat and clothing. Bones were used for tools and hooks. Fish and fowl made for the finest of eating. The berries and nuts of the woods and the wild rice of the lakes and streams were also important foods. Stones were shaped into both tools and weapons. Before the coming of guns and powder, both peoples used spears and bows and arrows. Clay soil was used to fashion pottery and utensils. With the coming of the trader, all sorts of ironware, knives and trinkets became available. Metal soon replaced stone for arrowheads and was also used in other weapons. Indians took well to gardening. Pierre La Verendrye taught them how on Lake of the Woods in the 1730's and Simon Dawson was astounded to find an eight acre garden on an island in the Northwest Angle of the Lake of the Woods in 1857. The Sioux tribes apparently

OJIBWE LODGE   *SIOUX TEPEE*

In winter, two layers of hides and/or bark were used to provide insulation.

learned gardening on their own or from other tribes. Most of what the Indian took from his environment was for survival, but he did harvest one luxury — tobacco. In Minnesota, the chief ingredient came from the dried inner bark of the kinnikinic (red willow) which was often mixed with powdered leaves and roots from other plants. In the prairies, the wild tobacco plant was used by the various Sioux tribes. Pipes made from stone (catlinite)[5] taken from the quarries near Pipestone, Minnesota, were used by many tribes — often long distances from this source. Smoking also marked ceremonial occasions, much as toasting with alcoholic drinks has been customary for centuries on special occasions in other civilizations. The pipe also was (and is) an important part of worship. Smoke, like incense in other cultures, represents prayers to the Supreme Being.

Both tribes loved paint and feathers. Both were a singing and dancing people. They were gregarious and lovers of feasts and games. The Sioux particularly enjoyed "betting."

There were few differences in how the Sioux and Ojibwe made use of nature's bounty while residing in our state. Both, for example, harvested the sap from the maple tree and used it to make sugar. In late March or early April, the return of the first crow caused great rejoicing because it signaled the coming of spring and the rising of the sap in the maple trees. Winter hunting encampments would break up. The Crow Wing and the Long Prairie Rivers were favorite wintering locations for the Leech Lake Ojibwe. The families, relations and even whole villages would move to their traditional "sugar bush" area where they would stay until May. Permanent lodges were located at these sites. They were large, usually measuring from 10 to 20 feet wide and 25 to 40 feet long. Sometimes smaller, temporary huts were built — called "wig-wa-si-ga-mig" by the Ojibwe. Whites nicknamed them "wigwams." The trees were tapped by cutting a slash and driving a cedar splinter or carved spigot into the wood. The sap dripped off the splinter and was then collected in containers on the ground (made from birchbark). Syrup was made by boiling the sap for days over an open fire. Although the syrup was sometimes used for food, it was usually thickened by continued boiling and then when it was the right consistency, placed in a basswood trough where it was gently stirred until it became granulated, thus forming sugar. Before there were iron kettles, birch bark containers held the sap and hot stones were dropped into the liquid.

Often times the syrup was poured into molds and allowed to harden. This "hard sugar" could be stored more conveniently for use throughout the year. One family could prepare as much as 500 pounds of maple sugar in a single season. The hard sugar was eaten as a food or confection; granulated sugar was used as a seasoning or flavoring agent; and a beverage was made by dissolving the maple sugar in water.

Spring was also the time for fishing, trapping and hunting. In addition to using nets and traps, spawning fish were often speared at night with a birch bark or pine knot torch for light. Migratory waterfowl were again found on the Indian menu. Muskrats were easier to trap. All in all, spring was a time for both work and rejoicing. Celebrations, feasting and reli-

Syrup was made by boiling sap for days over an open fire.

Courtesy of the Minnesota Historical Society

gious ceremonies accompanied the spring activities.

July and August were a season for berry picking. The braves may have been helpful in locating the berry patches, but the women and children did the picking. Just as today, the woodlands then had an abundance of blueberries, chokecherries, pincherries, raspberries, strawberries, and cranberries (both low and high bush). Every effort was made to preserve the fruit for use later in the year. Some berries were dried whole; others were dried and then pulverized. Boiling was sometimes used, particularly with raspberries. Pemmican, a Sioux favorite, was made by mixing dried berries with animal fat and stuffing the mixture into animal intestine casings. It was also at this time that ducks and geese became quite helpless during a period of molting and young birds were taken just before they were large enough to fly. Unsportsmanlike? Not when you're talking about food for survival!

September brought the wild rice harvest and another occasion to feast and celebrate. It was perhaps even a greater time for reunions and socializing than the sugar camps. Most harvesting was done by the women, usually two to a canoe. While one paddled or poled the boat through the rice bed, the other sat in front and pulled the rice over the canoe, beating the heads with a stick – thus dislodging the mature kernels. Since all of the

Ojibwe Scalp Dance–from watercolor by Peter Rindisbacker in West Point Museum. White explorers were impressed with the muscular physique of Native Americans, early drawings made them look like Greek Athletes!

rice in each head did not mature at the same time, the harvesters could cover the same area several times a few days apart.

The kernels were further separated from the husks by beating or trampling and then the chaff was blown away by throwing the rice into the air on a windy day. The kernels were then parched by the fire.

The same animals that are found in Minnesota today were here centuries ago – plus a few more. The earliest inhabitants of our state found such huge beasts as the woolly mammoth and the giant bison. Buffalo, caribou and elk were common in Minnesota – even after white men first arrived. Most animals, such as moose, were probably more plentiful than today, but others, such as deer, may have been less plentiful. But for all of the animal life, hunting was not always easy. Such primitive weapons as spears and bows and arrows gave wild game a great advantage. Predators and disease probably took a greater toll than the Indians, and severe winters were hard on both the hunter and the hunted.

Although there were few differences in how the Ojibwe and the Dakotas made use of nature's bounty, in some ways the tribes were not alike. Language was perhaps the most significant difference. Even though several tribes of the Algonquins and the Sioux had been neighbors for centuries, even the basic root words bore no resemblance. It is likely that the ancestors of these two tribes migrated to North America at different periods of history and from different parts of Asia. Differences in facial and other physical characteristics were accented by diverse clothing, head gear, and hair styles. As mentioned earlier, the Sioux were of a tall but athletic build, while the Ojibwe were more stocky but sturdy. White explorers were impressed with the muscular physique of the Native Americans; early drawings made them look like Greek athletes!

Both tribes were very religious, but there were significant differences as well as similarities.

Both believed in a Supreme Being or Great Spirit. Both believed in a life after death. Both had a multitude of lesser gods or spirits — usually taken from nature. The Sioux labeled the spirits or the unknown as "waken;" The Ojibwe called them "manitou." Religion called for such virtues as patience, truth and honesty, but curses were called down upon enemies. Superstitions and religious legends were numerous and varied somewhat from tribe to tribe and village to village. Gods were worshipped in prayers, offerings, chants and dances. The Ojibwe in particular, were conscientious about offering prayers whenever food was harvested or taken in a hunt. Visions and dreams were generated by fasting and meditation. Tobacco was often offered as a sacrifice.

"The happy hunting ground" was a place where the Indian was free from his struggle for survival and all the necessities of life were easily attained. Chief Bemidji described the Indian's "Hell" as a place where the hungry Indian could see hundreds of walleyes through six feet of ice with no way to cut through, or a deer was always just going over the second hill as he came over the first, or he was very cold and all the wood was too wet to start a fire.

Medicine men were both priests and healers. When herbs or other medicines did not work they exorcised evil spirits. They practiced the "laying on of hands" to invoke a blessing.

The help of the gods was sought before each serious endeavor, whether it be waging war, hunting or whatever.

Dances often included a religious or other serious purpose and were

Chief Bemidji. He was not really a chief but was well liked and highly respected by all. He lived where the Mississippi enters Lake Bemidji. The word "Bemidji" is an Ojibwe word meaning "a lake that has a river running through it."

not performed merely as entertainment.

The Ojibwe had a religious-cultural hero named "Nanabozho," who created the world for the Indian and taught him about the Great Spirit and religious practices. The practices were called "Midewiwin," and they were characterized by secret ceremonies and initiations including a guardian spirit for each and a "totem" spirit for each family group or relation. The Ojibwe had about twenty totems with as many as 1,000 members in a totem family. It was taboo for members of the same totem to marry. There were a few examples of the totem practice among Sioux tribes but it is believed that these can be traced in each case to intermarriages with the Ojibwe. The totem was symbolized by a bird, animal, reptile or fish. In addition, each Ojibwe carried a medicine bag which contained herbs and items such as shells which represented special powers and protection. The priests were called "Mides."

Polygamy was permitted by both tribes with the male taking more than one wife. Because so many were killed in battle, this was necessary to maintain the population.

Upon death, following a ceremony and appropriate mourning, bodies were sometimes bundled on scaffolds or placed in trees — particularly during the cold time of the year — and buried later. The Ojibwe traditionally buried their dead in a sitting position facing west. A long, low house–like shelter was constructed over the grave. Food was placed here along with all the deceased would need in the way of tools and weapons to help in the journey westward "across the river" to an eternal reward. A carved or drawn symbol of the appropriate totem was often placed outside the shelter.

In the novel "White Indian Boy[7]" by this author, we are given a look at a Midewiwin ceremony through the eyes of young Johnny Tanner, hero of the book:

In the years to come, Johnny would have many pleasant memories associated with the months the family would spend at Rainy Lake and

Courtesy of the Heartland Historical Society

Ojibwe "spirit houses" near Old Agency Bay, on the Onigum Peninsula of Leech Lake.

over those years he would return again and again to visit the village. Among the more interesting of those memories would be his exposure to several new facets of Ojibwe religion and tradition.

Shortly after Net-no-kwa (Johnny's mother) and the boys arrived at the village, the very secret and mysterious Midewinin ceremony was held. The ever-curious Johnny heard about the preparations and had many questions for his new brother-in-law, beginning with "What is the purpose of the ceremony? Is it something a person belongs to?"

"Whoa, Little Falcon[7]—one question at a time." Maji-go-bo replied. "Yes, it is a secret society people belong to, but because it is secret there isn't a great deal I am permitted to tell you. However, it is common knowledge among all Indians that its purpose is to help its members stay in good health, heal them when they are sick, and make it possible for them to enjoy long life."

"Are you a member, Maji-go-bo?"

"Yes, I was initiated several years ago."

"Can anybody join?" Johnny asked.

"I guess so, but you must ask to be admitted. One becomes eligible to apply if he is healed by a member of the society or if he has a vision or a dream in which the Great Spirit makes it clear that he should seek membership."

"Is the chief the leader?" was the next question.

"No, the society is run by the medicine men; they are called "Mides". You will be allowed to witness the ceremonies and the Mides will be the ones who direct the proceedings."

At this point Maji-go-bo stopped talking, so Johnny prodded him with, "Tell me more."

"There really isn't much more I am allowed to tell you, except, maybe, that there are "degrees" of accomplishment or honors one may attain— four of them in all—but I cannot tell you anything more about them. I understand other lodges have eight degrees and it is said degrees are

Ojibwe mourners

A Midewiwin Lodge

sometimes taught beyond the customary four or eight, but those often teach black magic. Some of these evil Mides who teach additional degrees are called "Bear Walkers" because they are said to go about at night disguised in a bear skin taking vengeance on their enemies."

Johnny's curiosity was really piqued by this time, but he knew it would be improper to pursue the inquiry further.

On the first day of the ceremony Maji-go-bo took Wa-me-gon-a-biew, (Johnny's Indian brother) and Johnny with him to witness the big event.

As they drew near the far side of the village, Johnny was surprised to see an enormous lodge, about 200 feet long, approximately 30 feet wide, and maybe 10 feet high. It was constructed in the same manner as the lodges the Indians lived in, with the larger end of small trees set into the ground and the tops bent over and lashed together in the middle. But just the framework was there, there was no hide or bark covering and the spectators could see all that went on inside. However, only the members or those about to join were admitted into the enclosure.

Courtesy of the Crow Wing County Historical Society

A birch scroll depicting the Midewiwin ceremony. Note the clam shell right of center. The clam was an important Ojibwe symbol. Some believe its significance can be traced to the generations of Ojibwe who lived by the Atlantic Ocean. Some current scholars also suggest that as the tribes followed the receding glaciers north, the ice cap in the distance may have resembled a clam.

As the participants arrived, some carried drums of skin stretched over hollow sections of logs or across a wooden circular frame, others carried rattles. Many had pipes, and still others carried what looked like scrolls of birchbark. "What do you suppose those birchbark rolls are for?" Johnny asked his brother.

"I don't know but I understand there are pictures and symbols written on them that have some magical meaning," Wa-me-gon-a-biew replied.

The initiates stood in a separate group as they arrived, but before they were allowed to enter the big lodge they had to first take a steam bath in a small hut close to the lake as sort of a purification ceremony. Water was splashed on very hot rocks and the people stayed inside as long as

*they could stand the steam. When they could take no more they would
dash to the water's edge and dive in.*

*Noticing that some were very young, Johnny asked Wa-me-gon-a-biew,
"Why don't you belong to the lodge?"*

*"Midewinin practices were not common where we used to live," he
replied.*

*The purging completed, the initiates approached the enclosure and
the ceremony commenced. Those who were already members were the
first to enter the lodge—following the medicine men, and led by the chief
priest. Each initiate brought a dead dog which he lay in front of the
entrance and which he had to step over as he entered the lodge. The
dogs would later be roasted and eaten during the ceremony. As a part
of the ritual, present lodge members stood around the doorway and
tried to dissuade the new members from entering. However, each initiate looked neither to the right nor to the left but kept his eyes straight
ahead on the medicine pole which had been erected as the focal point
in the enclosure. The new members also carried gifts for the Mides; the
higher the degree they were seeking, the more valuable the gift. The hundred or more occupants of the lodge followed the leadership of the
priests—dancing, singing, shaking their rattles, beating their drums and
repeating secret words and phrases as they paraded around the inside
of the enclosure. After more than an hour of these preliminary activities, everyone sat down in their previously assigned positions. Later in
the day the new members were initiated.*

*For the boys, the most intriguing part of the ceremony was when the
Mides pretended to shoot snail and clam shells into the bodies of the
new members. Each pretended to be struck down as though dead but
then with the encouragement of the medicine men made believe they
were coughing up the shells into their hands. These shells were supposed to have great magical and protective powers and were placed in
their medicine pouches for safe keeping.*

In the same book, "White Indian Boy," Johnny experiences the traditional Ojibwe ritual through which a boy enters manhood:

*Net-no-kwa, Johnny's Indian mother, made the arrangements and a
few days hence Maji-go-bo, Johnny's' brother-in-law, huddled with his
new protégé. He explained the rules. First he must blacken his face with
charcoal, and then spend 10 days alone in the bush without eating or
speaking to anyone he might chance to see. "And you must pray each
day," he added, "petitioning the Great Spirit to show you your guardian
spirit through a vision or a dream."*

*"This is a good time to ask me any other questions you would ask
your father if he were here, about Indian ways or about growing into
being a brave."*

Never short on words, Johnny responded with a barrage of questions as though he might never again have the opportunity to ask an adult about anything. Only bedtime and complete weariness on Johnny's part saved Maji-go-bo from the marathon of inquiries.

After a day of stuffing himself with food almost to the point of becoming ill, Johnny took to the woods. The first three days were uneventful—but miserable. Johnny was tempted to eat even the buds on the trees, but he held firm to his commitment. By the third day, water seemed to satisfy his hunger pangs. He slept as much as he could, thus helping the time to pass and at the same time conserving his strength. The nights were the toughest. Johnny had never heard so many night sounds. He didn't mind the loons on the far off lake or the owls up in the tree tops, but raccoons, deer and other night creatures made suspicious noises as they moved through the dry leaves still on the ground from the previous autumn. At night a boy's imagination works overtime and he thought every raccoon was a skunk and every deer a lynx.

On the sixth morning, Johnny walked down to a stream for a drink of water, but found someone there before him—a cow moose and her twin calves. They had not noticed his approach so he clapped his hands and shouted expecting the clumsy calves to fall over each other trying to escape. To his surprise all three just stared at him. When the mother located the source of the disturbance she shook her big head and pawed the shallow water where she stood, throwing mud and rocks into the brush behind her. That was enough for Johnny and he took off into the woods, but he could hear the monstrous animal in pursuit. He knew he couldn't outrun her so he stopped behind a substantial clump of birch trees. Mother moose had no hesitation in playing a game of "round the birches." A couple of times she reared up on her hind legs like a horse as though to trample her young adversary. In Johnny's weakened condition he knew he couldn't keep this up much longer so he scampered up the largest of the trees. When the moose understood his move she gave him a boost with her nose—but the help was purely accidental; she really didn't want him out of her reach. The huge beast continued to make threatening motions with her head and hooves, but Johnny was safely out of harm's way. Just when she seemed to be calming down, the calves showed up and she again worked herself into a frenzy. After what seemed like hours the moose gave up and led her calves away.

When Johnny was sure he was safe he crawled down and stretched. Then, as though she had been waiting in ambush, the moose thundered back on the scene. Johnny retreated up the tree, and none too soon. And so there was a repeat performance of pawing and head shaking and brushing against the clump of trees. She didn't stay nearly as long as the first time, but again when Johnny descended she was back. This

*time he had kept one hand on a substantial branch and the moose was-
n't even close by the time he was 10 feet up in the air. Apparently the
animal's anger and frustration finally turned to discouragement
because this time she left for good. Johnny spent the rest of the day very
close to trees he could climb and come dark he built himself a cradle like
platform in another clump of birches. There was no way he would sleep
on the ground with the moose and her calves in the vicinity!*

*Before going to sleep, Johnny again prayed that he could be given a
guardian spirit. As he finally dozed off he was thinking, "It would be just
my luck to dream about a moose; after all the trouble they've given me
I don't think I could trust a moose spirit to be on my side."*

*Shortly after he fell asleep, Johnny moved just right—or just wrong—
and awoke with a crash as he landed on the ground flat on his back! He
was sure the moose had him. But when there was no attack he finally
figured out what had happened and crawled back up to his cradle. This
time it was nearly daybreak when he finally dozed off once again. As
the sun rose he was still fast asleep. A crow alighted in his tree and
began an awful racket—all of which triggered a dream in Johnny's tired
brain. He thought he had once again fallen to the ground and the moose
calves were attacking him. In his dream he heard crows cawing and
imagined that dozens of the big black birds drove off the moose calves
and carried him with their beaks to the top of a big pine tree and safe-
ty. Then he dreamed he was falling....falling...falling down through the
branches; as he regained consciousness he realized he actually was
falling! but this time he was awake enough to grab at the branches as
they passed by and broke his fall, actually landing on his feet. As he
stood there, leaning against a tree trunk for support and trying to catch
his breath, he suddenly realized, "Hey! I've had my dream! The crow is
my guardian spirit!"*

*All that day Johnny searched for a crow feather to put in the deerskin
medicine pouch Net-no-kwa had given him before he left the village. He
saw several crows' nests but no feathers were to be found on the ground
below. Then he had an idea, why not climb one of those trees? There
would surely be some feathers in a nest. He retraced his steps to the last
one he had seen—in a huge red pine with the nest well up towards the
top. After resting a considerable time to regain his strength, he began
the climb. The possibility of young ones being in the nest had never
occurred to him. About half way up an adult crow discovered him and
cried out in alarm. Crows came from every where—dozens of them.
Their cawing was deafening as they took turns diving at Johnny, coming so close he could easily have hit or kicked several, but he just held
on for dear life. Suddenly one of the crows landed in the nest, killed the
half grown young one that was there, and pushed it out! The fluttering*

of the dead bird to the ground was like a signal. The cawing ceased and every crow flew away. Almost sadly, Johnny slid down and picked up the dead bird. Staring at the lifeless form he rationalized, "Maybe it was meant to be."

Anyway, the quest was over. Taking his knife from his belt, Johnny cut off one claw. Then he plucked the longest feather from a wing, and placed both items in his medicine pouch. He was a brave!

In his book, "Indian Days" the late Carl Zapffe, scientist and historian, gives the following description of the powers of a "jeesaki" (the name given leading medicine men who were also prophets):

We can take a quick look at one of the numerous published descriptions of awe—inspiring Jeesaki ceremonies which should at least settle the claim that the phenomena are real, not fraudulent, and thus far beyond scientific explanation. The record appears in a publication of the Smithsonian Institution. The time: 1858; place: Leech Lake; and the purpose in this case was not to secure other world aid for some situation of human need, but this time simply to prove other—world intervention as factual. On the other hand, perhaps this can be classed as a human need.

Be that as it may, the widely renowned Government Interpreter Paul Beaulieu, it seems, had challenged a local Jeesaki, placing $100 on a wager that the man could not perform to the satisfaction of himself and a committee of twelve men including the resident Episcopal clergyman. Beaulieu prepared a list of several "crucial tests" allowing the Jeesaki to select any one of them that he wished. Which he did.

Poles were cut, sunk deeply into the ground, and on a slant allowing about a 10-inch hole at the top for "Spirit entry". Cross staves were then lashed to the frame to make the special kind of shelter called a Jeesakan; and this was then completely covered with blankets and birchbark except for a tiny flap door, so small that no man could get in or out without assistance. The Jeesaki was tied with a strong rope, and by Beaulieu himself, who began by pulling a tight knot around his ankles, next winding the rope behind the knees and forward to tie both wrists. Laying the man's arms atop his bent knees, he then passed a billet of wood through the gap between the backside of the knees and the foreside of his elbows; roped all of this to the knees and arms while making four passes around his neck; then pulled on it until agreement on the part of the committee was unanimous that the man could never possibly escape — no way! Even the several hundred onlookers thought it a bit overdone. The only way they could get him into the shelter was to lay the man on a small mat and push him through the little doorway. Meantime no objections were raised by the Jeesaki to any of this, though he did enter one request: He needed his Sacred Pipe and Sacred Stone with him — a polished chunk of black basalt. Would they please slide them beneath his body before closing the flap?

This they did. His chants and prayers began; and almost immediately there were loud thumping noises; several voices could be heard inside; none in a recognizable language; the Jeesakan began swaying with rapidly increasing violence – and the Episcopal Priest quickly got the Hell out of there! Forgetting the glossolalia and related phenomena in his own church history, this man was now fully convinced that Satan was behind it all, and that "this was not the place for him!"

Scarcely had he cleared the site, however, and retreated over the hill, when the ruckus began calming down. Then a voice was heard which clearly did belong to the Jeesaki:

"Mr. Beaulieu, go to your home and get your rope!"

Since every care had been taken to protect such things even as confederacy between the Jeesaki and some member of the committee, Beaulieu now cautioned them to let no man approach the shelter until he returned. Soon he was back. In his hands was the rope, all knots still tied! Beaulieu had lost the bet.

William Warren, the Ojibwe author we have previously quoted, was a self-ordained Christian missionary. He told in his "History of the Ojibways" something about his efforts to convert his people to Christianity. He was surprised that the elders of the tribes often knew the Old Testament stories of the Bible – but identified the heroes with Indian names. This led him to speculate that the Indian people could have been descendants of the "Ten Lost Tribes of Israel!"[8]

As we conclude this chapter with its descriptions of the cultures of the Dakota Sioux and the Ojibwe, we might speculate where their villages were located on Leech Lake. First, we must remember that the lake was inhabited off and on for at least 4,000 years and it is therefore likely that there were village sites at some time on all or nearly all pieces of high and dry ground whether on points, bays or islands. However, since the lake level has been raised nearly seven feet by the dam on the Leech Lake River, we can assume that many of the early sites are now under water. We do know from the journals and records of explorers, traders and missionaries (and in some cases from eye–witnesses in the 1800s) that there were villages on Ottertail Point, Stony Point, the Hardwood Points, Battle (Sugar) Point, Oak (Squaw) Point, Bear Island, Shingobee Island, the site of Walker, Waboose Bay and the outlet of Leech Lake River, the north narrows on Ottertail Point, the first high ground on both sides of the mouth of the Sucker River and Onigum. That is not to say that there were villages at all these sites simultaneously.

Drawing on Elden Johnson's report to the Corps of Engineers in 1979 entitled, "Cultural Resources Investigation of the Reservoir Shorelines of

Gull Lake, Leech Lake, Pine River and Lake Pokegema" and reports of local land owners, the following sites on the shores of Leech Lake provided a significant number of artifacts to indicate possible village sites; including:

Bear Island (including 7 mounds)

Battle (Sugar) Point

northernmost high ground on west side of Sucker Bay (owner of cabin had literally buckets of artifacts)

Bear Trap Point (across from Pine Point)

Steamboat Bay (east side across from Minnesota Island and several other sites)

small island to the west of Waboose point at outlet of Waboose Bay into Portage Bay

Blackduck Point (Boy Bay)

Long Point (north end of Portage Bay)

Five Mile Point (also the site of an American Fur Co. Trading Post)

large island at the north end of Uram Bay

Uram Bay shoreline, both eastern point and southwest high ground

small island to the west of Partridge Point

Waboose Bay, high ground

Portage Bay, west side across from Five Mile Point

Headwaters Bay, northeast side

Chippewa Bay

Pipe Island, east shore

Ottertail Point, including extreme southern tip, extreme southwest side, southeast side, north side of "Ottertail Island" and several sites along the east side of Sucker Bay

Baumgard's Landing, north of state lots on west side of Sucker Bay (also the site of an early logging camp)

south of state lots on east side of Sucker Bay (sometimes called Ricebed Point)

Oak Point (formerly Squaw Point)

Hardwood Point

Little Hardwood Point

Walker Bay, west side and north end of Cedar Point

Shingobee Island, south point

Agency Narrows, northeast point and other high ground

Agency Bay, southeast side

between Walker Bay and Agency Narrows

Johnson listed several other sites where just a few artifacts were found. These may or may not have been village sites. It is interesting (but not surprising) that many sites produced artifacts of more than one culture.

Again we must remember that the present level of Leech Lake is about 7 feet higher than before the dam was constructed. It is very likely that additional village sites are now flooded.

There were probably less than ten major villages at any one time during the Ojibwe occupation. The small islands sometimes served as summer camps.

Each major village had its own chief (usually hereditary) and governance. Some villages had different civil and war chiefs. Since all of the villages on the lake at any one time were all Dakota Sioux or all Ojibwe, it is doubtful that there was serious conflict between villages, but we know this sometimes happened on other lakes (such as Gull Lake) so that certainly wasn't impossible. We also know that on Leech Lake at the time of the "last Indian War," there was not unanimous active support for Chief "Bug" (some leaders were neutral).

Certain chiefs were recognized as "principal chiefs" by the United States government. They were usually thus recognized because Native Americans in that area accepted them as most influential or "greatest" and because white traders or explorers evaluated them as most important. Chief Flat Mouth, the elder, was recognized by Native Americans and whites as principal chief of not only Leech Lake but also of the entire north central part of what is now Minnesota. Following his death, the power appears to have been shared by his son, Flat Mouth the younger, Chief Buffalo, Chief Big Dog and Majigabo II who was chief of the Bear Island Indians.

In summary, it was the Dakota Sioux who took control of Leech Lake in the 1600's and remained in undisputed control until 1739. From 1739 to 1766, Leech Lake was a part of Minnesota's "no man's land". It was a time when it was impossible to establish permanent villages. Both Dakota Sioux and Ojibwe war parties roamed the woodlands. Few white traders entered the woodlands during those years. Not only was there an element of danger, but with all the fighting there was little time to trap, so few furs were available.

It was in 1766 that an army of Ojibwe invaded the woodlands from the east and soundly defeated the Dakotas. From that time on, permanent villages were established by the Ojibwe on Leech and other woodland lakes. Thus, when the first white explorers, traders and missionaries reached Leech Lake, they found the Ojibwe firmly in control.

[1]Those living in the area we now call Minnesota are usually referred to as Dakotas; those living in what are now parts of North and South Dakota east of the Missouri as the Nakota and those west of the Missouri as the Lakota.

[2]The tribe was originally referred to as "Chippewa". In later years, "Ojibwe" became more popular. Today, many use "Anishinaubay."

[3]LaPointe was occupied by the Hurons and the Ottawas for about twenty years prior to the take over by the Ojibwe.

[4]Although it was the Nakotas from the prairies of what is now North Dakota who attacked the French, it was the Dakota Sioux of what is now Minnesota who were the targets of revenge.

[5]Named for George Catlin, an artist and explorer who claimed to be the discoverer of the pipestone quarries. Others were actually there before him but he originally received the credit.

[6]The real John Tanner was kidnapped from his missionary parents in Ohio and raised in the Minnesota-Ontario boundary waters area by Ottawa Indians. As an adult, he was an important leader of his adopted people. He was associated with men like Lord Selkirk (head of the Hudson's Bay Co.) and Henry Schoolcraft (Discoverer of the source of the Mississippi River).

[7]John's Indian name.

[8]A theory also held by the Mormon faith.

CHAPTER III
The 100 Year
Dakota Sioux – Ojibwe War

In the last chapter we saw how the Sioux-Ojibwe contest for control of the northern Minnesota woodlands began in the 1730s. The great victories of the Ojibwe and their allies in 1766 did not end the conflict; it continued with few interruptions up to the time of the Civil War.

If we consider this in the perspective of the history of the United States, the conflict began 40 years before the start of the Revolutionary War and ended during the Civil War! Four generations of fighting. In 1862, following the white-Sioux conflict in the Mankato-New Ulm area, the military drove the Sioux out of the state into the Dakotas and Canada, thus ending the potential for fighting between the Ojibwe and the Sioux. During the more than 100 years of fighting, the Ojibwe war parties were made-up of warriors from all of the major lakes of the northern Minnesota woodlands–from the Canadian border down to Mille Lacs Lake. Leech Lake braves, however, seemed to be involved in nearly all of the major battles. Although the Cree were ahead of the Ojibwe in establishing villages on Leech Lake after the Sioux fled, they moved back north into Canada after a relative short stay on the lake.

The following are some of the major battles in which the Leech Lake Ojibwe participated during the 100 year war with the Dakota Sioux:

The Battle at the Mouth of the Crow Wing

It was 1768. The Dakota Sioux had been driven from their strongholds in northern Minnesota but had not given up. They had even been forced from their Mille Lacs Lake headquarters village when the Ojibwe blew up their earthen houses by dropping gunpowder down the smoke holes. It was from their new headquarters village at the mouth of the Rum River that a small army of about 200 braves launched a raid against the new Ojibwe capital on Sandy Lake.

At the same time, an Ojibwe war party of about seventy men moved south down the Mississippi with the Rum River village as their objective.

The Dakotas proceeded up the Mississippi (but chose to take the Crow Wing cutoff), then traveled up the Gull River, across Gull, Long and Whitefish Lakes, then up to Pine River and across a series of lakes leading to Boy River and Leech Lake—on the way to Sandy Lake (probably because there was less current to fight). Thus the two war parties did not meet on their way to their respective objectives.

Apparently the Ojibwe did not find any indication that the Dakota Sioux had traveled up the Mississippi river only days before. They were surprised to find the Rum River village deserted, with the women and children safely protected elsewhere. Surprise turned to horror when the Ojibwe realized the possible significance of the empty village. Their worst fears were to be realized. The Dakotas had fallen on the helpless Sandy Lake village and slaughtered everyone except thirty young women whom they took captive along with an older woman to care for them. The Ojibwe wasted no time looking for the hidden Dakota Sioux women and children but hurried back up river—intent on finding a battlefield of their liking to ambush the Sioux. They reached the mouth of the Crow Wing without encountering the enemy, and here they finally discovered camp signs left by the Dakotas on their way north. They dared go no further because they were not sure on which river the Sioux would come—the Crow Wing or the Mississippi. They quickly dug in on a bluff on the east bank of the Mississippi overlooking both rivers (where their excavations may be seen to this day as a part of Crow Wing State Park). They did not have long to wait. A scout reported that the Dakota Sioux war party was on its way down the Mississippi. They stopped across from Crow Wing Island, where they forced their captives to serve them breakfast, in full view of their loved ones who were anxiously lying in ambush.

As the story goes, the old woman whose life had been spared to care for the captives turned out to be a real heroine. She had quietly reminded her charges that there was a good chance they would meet the returning men from their village somewhere along the river. If and when this should happen, she urged the women to overturn the canoes and swim towards the rifle fire. And that is exactly what happened. The unsuspecting Dakotas were caught completely off guard and suffered heavy casualties. The Ojibwe had chosen their battleground well. Here the Mississippi narrowed and made a sharp turn, the faster current bringing the Dakota Sioux into close range, but they were not about to give up their captives or leave without a good fight. Incensed over the sudden turn of events and the fact they had been outsmarted by their captives—women at that (Indian warriors of that time were real male chauvinists!)—they placed the Ojibwe under siege. When frontal attacks proved too costly, they crossed the river and circled behind them on land, but the Ojibwe were too well protected and continued to get the better of the battle. At last, the

Dakotas decided "discretion was indeed the better part of valor" and reluctantly turned their canoes downstream.

A Truce

The only significant truce during the 100 Years War took place around the 1770s when the Ojibwe and the Dakota Sioux agreed to hunt and trap in peace during the winter months in the area around the Long Prairie and the Crow Wing Rivers.

These hunting grounds were so important to both the Sioux and the Ojibwe that when neither was able to conclusively drive the other from it, a winter truce was negotiated several years running. Prior to this time, a hunter might very well return to his camp at night with a scalp or two hanging from his belt as well as furs taken during the day. The truce also made it possible to take the entire family on the winter hunt.

So good was the hunting that the Ojibwe came from as far away as Leech Lake and Sandy Lake; these villages retained a close relationship over the years and it was their custom to rendezvous at Gull Lake or the mouth of the Crow Wing on their way to the winter hunting grounds. The Mille Lacs Ojibwe also wintered in the Crow Wing–Long Prairie areas.

The virgin pine forests of the north were not good habitat for wildlife because insufficient light could filter through to nourish the undergrowth which provides food for both birds and animals. Because of the scarcity of game in the Winter and the thick ice covering the lakes, it made sense to move to the edge of the prairies where food and furs were more readily available. The Sioux came from as far away as the prairies of present day North and South Dakota and included the Wahpetons and Sissetons as well as other Dakota bands. They were probably drawn by the beaver.

The Ojibwe bands from Leech, Sandy and other lakes then traveled up the Long Prairie and Crow Wing Rivers. They were especially attracted by the herds of elk and buffalo that grazed in the area, as well as the beaver in the streams. The Dakotas were usually there first and already settled in their hide–covered teepees. After warring back and forth all summer, the only way the Ojibwe could be certain the winter truce would again be in effect was to directly approach the Sioux village and offer to smoke the pipe of peace. Dressed for the occasion and well-armed, a vanguard — not so large as to be threatening but not so small as to be easy prey — would march right into the Sioux village. The bearer of the peace pipe and the banner carriers led the procession. The customary response of the Dakotas was to welcome the Ojibwe with a volley of rifle fire. Sometimes the singing bullets were so near the ears of the visitors that it seemed the "name of the game" was to come as close as possible without scoring! Once it was clear that a truce was desired, the Ojibwe were welcomed into the lodges of the Sioux where they smoked the peace pipe and feasted on the best available food—sometimes literally beneath the scalps of their fellow tribesmen which may have been taken as recently as the past summer and now hung suspended from the lodge poles. The Ojibwe had a word for this ceremony; they called it "Pin-ding-u-daud-e-win," which is translated, "to enter into one another's lodges."

An interesting custom during these periods of truce was for warriors to adopt "brothers" from among the traditional enemies of the other tribes. Often they were considered as replacements for special friends or brothers lost in battle. There are many tales of adopted brothers being spared during subsequent raids or battles. It is told that the relationship between the two tribes sometimes became so friendly that there was intermarrying and even the exchanging of wives.

The End of the Truce — Chief Yellow Hair's Revenge

Chief Flat Mouth of Leech Lake was the most able and significant leader of the Ojibwe in the 1800s. We will speak much more of him shortly. His father, Wa-son-aun-e-qua or "Yellow Hair," however, was somewhat of a scoundrel. According to Flat Mouth, Chief Yellow Hair did not inherit his title, but achieved his leadership role through a remarkable knowledge of medicines, including poisons. It is said that his enemies lost their lives in a mysterious and unaccountable manner. His own son called him "vindictive" and "revengeful" and said that he retaliated against his enemies two-fold. It is likely that Yellow Hair was a follower of a well known false prophet or "Shaman" of that day. This medicine man turned witch doctor garnered a tremendous following among the Ojibwe and persuaded them to forsake their traditional Midewiwin religion. He claimed to have a new revelation from the Great Spirit and urged all to throw away their little medicine bags and follow him. A religious rally of sorts was held at the location of present day Detroit. However, when it was discovered he could not raise the dead some of his followers had brought to him and when he was found hiding in a hollow tree when he was supposed to be in heaven conferring with the Great Spirit, his disciples (including Yellow Hair and Flat Mouth) deserted him.

Typical of Yellow Hair's vengeful spirit is this story of how the Winter truce between the Sioux and the Ojibwe was broken:

As we have mentioned, the Ojibwe and Dakota Sioux had entered into a truce so that they could hunt and trap in peace during the winter in the Crow Wing—Long Prairie Rivers area. We have also stated that to cement the truce, it had become the custom of individual warriors to adopt one another from different tribes as brothers. Yellow Hair and a Dakota Sioux warrior adopted each other and became friends. Yellow Hair, who already spoke some Sioux, perfected his mastery of the tongue. In the spring, just before their return to Leech Lake, four Ojibwe children, including Yellow Hair's eldest son, (Flat Mouth's brother) were murdered while at play by a marauding band of Sioux from the west.

Yellow Hair urged revenge. His followers and other Ojibwe chiefs felt this would be useless because the war party was long gone. Yellow Hair, however, argued for revenge against any available Sioux, including those with whom they had a peace treaty. Others urged moderation, and the chief finally agreed to return to Leech Lake with the bodies of the children. After burial, however, Yellow Hair and five of his warriors headed back for the Long Prairie River, intent upon revenge. They encountered the Sandy Lake band who were on their way home. The leadership of this group perceived Yellow Hair's purpose and tried to dissuade him, knowing that a resumption of hostilities would escalate making it impossible to hunt and trap in peace during future winters. They even gave him more than enough gifts to "cover" the death of his son. Yellow Hair accepted the gifts and pretended to return to Leech Lake. However, when they were out of sight, he again turned southwest.

William Warren in his *"History of the Ojibways"* described the eventual gratification of Yellow Hair's loss thus:

On the head waters of Crow River, nearly two hundred miles from the point of his departure, Yellow Hair at last caught up with the two lodges of his enemies. At the first peep of dawn in the morning, the Dakotas were startled from their quiet slumbers by the fear-striking Ojibwe war—whoop, and as the men arose to grasp their arms and the women and children jumped up in affright, the bullets of the enemy fell amongst them, causing wounds and death. After the first moments of surprise, the men of the Dakotas returned the fire of the enemy, and for many minutes the fight raged hotly.

An interval in the incessant firing at last took place, and the voice of a Dakota, apparently wounded, called out to the Ojibways, "Alas! why is it that I die? I thought my road was clear before and behind me, and that the skies were cloudless above me. My mind dwelt only on good and blood was not in my thoughts."

Yellow Hair recognized the voice of the warrior who had agreed to be his adopted brother during the late peace between their respective tribes. He understood his words, but his wrong was great, and his heart had become as hard as flint. He answered: "My brother, I too thought that the skies were cloudless above me, and I lived without fear; but a wolf came and destroyed my young; he traced from the country of the Dakotas. My brother, for this you die!"

"My brother, I knew it not," answered the Dakota—" it was none of my people, but the wolves of the prairies."

*The Ojibwe warrior now quietly filled and lit his pipe, and while
he smoked, the silence was only broken by the groans of the wounded and the suppressed wail of bereaved mothers. Having finished
his smoke, he laid aside his pipe and once more he called out to the
Dakotas:*

*"My brother, have you still in your lodge a child who will take the
place of my lost one, whom your wolves have devoured? I have
come a great distance to behold once more my young as I once
beheld him, and I return not on my tracks till I am satisfied!"*

*The Dakotas, thinking that he wished for a captive to adopt
instead of his deceased child, and happy to escape certain destruction at such a cheap sacrifice, took one of the surviving children, a
little girl, and decking it with such finery and ornaments as they
possessed, they sent her out to the covet of the Ojibwe warrior. The
innocent little girl came forward, but no sooner was she within
reach of the avenger, than he grasped her by the hair of the head
and loudly exclaiming—"I sent for thee that I might do with you as
your people did to my child. I wish to behold thee as I once beheld
him," he deliberately scalped her alive, and sent her shrieking back
to her agonized parents.*

*After this cold—blooded act, the fight was renewed with great fury.
Yellow Hair rushed desperately forward, and by main force he
pulled down one of the Dakota lodges. As he did so the wounded
warrior, his former adopted brother, discharged his gun at his
breast, which the active and wary Ojibwe adroitly dodged, the con-
tents killed one of his comrades who had followed him close at his
back. Not a being in that Dakota lodge survived; the other, being
bravely defended, was left standing; and Yellow Hair, with his four
surviving companions, returned homeward, their vengeance fully
glutted, and having committed a deed which ever after became the
topic of the lodge circles of their people.*

Fortunately, Flat Mouth differed in may ways from his father. The practice of using poisons, for example, was abandoned once he succeeded him
as chief.

Ukkewaus' War Party — Poorly Conceived, Poorly Executed

Uk-ke-waus was not really a chief but he led a reluctant band of forty-
five Leech Lake warriors on a raid of Sioux villages in the Leaf Lakes and
Battle Lake area. At the outset, the majority of Leech Lake Indians was
anxious to organize a war party against the Dakota Sioux. Jean Baptiste
Cadotte (son of the Cadotte who was one of the first men to have contact
with the Ojibwe) had established a trading post at Cass Lake. When the

Pillagers came to him for powder and shot, he persuaded them not to go on the warpath. However, when they returned to Leech Lake with some liquor, a wild celebration was held. The next morning, Uk-ke-waus dared the braves to follow him on a mission of revenge against the Dakota Sioux. Of the forty-five who answered his call, less than one-third returned. In a violent battle at Battle Lake (from which the lake received its name), Uk-ke-waus and all four of his sons were killed. He and his three oldest sons had fought to their deaths in a delaying action against a large number of Dakotas so that the handful of remaining Ojibwe might escape. It was said that the brave sacrifice was made because of the guilt Uk-ke-waus felt for his foolishness in organizing the war party.

This is another example of how far warriors would travel to wage war.

Dakotas Attack A French Trading Post
At The Mouth Of The Partridge River

This tale is also from the lips of Chief Flat Mouth (the elder) of the Leech Lake Ojibwe – and was told first hand to William Warren, the Ojibwe historian.

One winter, when Flat Mouth was a child and too young to bear arms (early 1780), he accompanied members of his tribe to the confluence of the Partridge (or Pena River) and the Crow Wing, where a French trader had constructed a post only that fall. The Ojibwe called the trader "Ah-wish-to-yah," which meant "Blacksmith." Several voyageurs were there with him at the time and together with the Pillager–Ojibwe hunters and trappers totaled about forty men working out of the post. Most of the Indians had brought their families with them, even though they knew there was a good chance of an encounter with Dakota Sioux hunters or even war parties. The trader was also aware of the danger, but a heavy population of beaver had drawn him there.

Expecting the worst, the men erected a log barricade around the post and the wigwams.

Late one night, ten of the Ojibwe hunters awakened those at the post with the alarming news that a sizable band of Dakotas were in the area. They had crossed their trail and identified them by the lingering smell of tobacco (which was distinctly different from the ground inner-bark of the kinnikinnick smoked by the Ojibwe). The Dakota Sioux were following a trail which would lead them to a small, defenseless camp of hunters. Craftily, the Ojibwe circled ahead of the Dakotas and crossed the trail, hoping to lure them to the more easily defended barricade at the trading post. The strategy worked. By the time the Dakota Sioux arrived, the barricade had been strengthened and nearly twenty men (French and Ojibwe) were ready for the attack.

The party of Dakota Sioux was large indeed — about two hundred braves — but whereas the men at the post were all armed with guns, the Dakota Sioux were forced to depend on bows and arrows and had only a half-dozen rifles among them.

The huge war party finally appeared on the bank across from the trading post. Confident in their numerical superiority, they leisurely put on their paint, feathers and other ornaments. Then, sounding their war whoops, they charged across the ice sending out a cloud of arrows into the fortification. But the defenders were well—protected and their rifle fire was devastating. No Dakota Sioux reached the barricade. With a change in strategy, the Dakotas began firing their arrows almost straight up, lobbing them — like mortar fire — into the compound. The shower of barbed missiles was more effective and two Ojibwe hunters were wounded seriously enough to take them out of action. Some took refuge in the post itself. But in the end, the rifles proved to be more than an equalizing factor and a frustrated Dakota Sioux war party — with a greatly diminished supply of arrows — finally recognized the futility of the situation.

Before leaving, they cut holes in the river ice and gave their dead a watery burial.[1]

Shortly after their departure, other hunters and trappers who had heard the shooting arrived at the post — about twenty reinforcements in all. Realizing that the Dakotas were nearly out of arrows, they wanted to press their advantage by pursuing them. The trader argued to the contrary and finally prevailed.

It is interesting that at this date, about 1780, the Dakotas had so few guns. It may have been that they came from the prairies farther west[2] and had, therefore, little opportunity to procure them.

Two Examples of Late 18th Century Battles Between The Ojibwes And The Dakota Sioux[3]

Great Marten (Keche-wa-bi-she-shi), one of Bi-aus-wa's great war chiefs who led many raids from the Sandy Lake—Leech Lake area against the Dakota Sioux, perhaps deserves more credit than any other man for maintaining Ojibwe control of the Minnesota lake region.

The first campaign — under Great Marten's leadership — originated at Sandy Lake and included about 120 braves. It would be fair to speculate that some of the warriors might have come from the Leech—Cass Lake area, inasmuch as it was customary to invite participation from neighboring villages when large parties were organized and the residents of these tribes were close allies. A runner was sometimes sent from village to village bearing something symbolic belonging to the leader, such as a pipe or tomahawk — along with an invitation to join the campaign.

By the time of this first incursion, the Mississippi had become the favorite warpath of the Ojibwe in their attempts to expand their frontiers to the south and make their lake region villages more safe from Dakota attack. As the war party proceeded down the river, Great Marten sent a canoe of scouts ahead and runners along each bank to make certain there would be no ambush. A short distance above the mouth of the Elk River, the scouts heard voices of the Dakota dialect. Quickly and silently they turned their canoe, moved in tight to the shoreline and worked their way back upstream without detection. When they came into sight of their main party they threw water up in the air with their paddles to signify danger and that the war party should turn in to the eastern bank. After quickly applying war paint and adorning their hair with eagle feathers, they ran in disorder through the wooded river bottoms until they came to the open prairie. Before them was a line of Dakota Sioux warriors in battle dress, apparently starting on the warpath against some northern Ojibwe destination. Great Marten's men, all "psyched-up" for battle, charged out onto the prairie. When the parties were in gun range of each other they opened fire. Because there was no cover, the only defense was to keep in motion. It must have been a spectacular sight — the painted and plumed bodies leaping continually from side to side — accented by war whoops and gun fire. Although the two bands were about equal in size, the late arriving Ojibwe kept pouring from the woods and the Dakotas, assuming they would soon be badly outnumbered, turned and fled, leaving behind their blankets and other paraphernalia they were carrying for their raid in the north. A running fight continued for about three miles, when the Dakota Sioux met a large party from another Dakota village, apparently on their way to join them in their campaign against the Ojibwe. Now the tide turned and Great Marten's braves took flight. Upon reaching a grove of oak trees they made a stand. The Dakota Sioux were without cover and dug holes in the ground (fox holes are not an innovation of our times) and so the battle continued. As the Dakotas tried to dig in closer they suffered numerous casualties. Then, noting a stiff south wind and the dry prairie grass killed during the recent winter, the Dakota Sioux set a fire. The Ojibwe were soon routed from the oak grove and lost three of their number to encircling flames. The prairie fire did, however, give them time to flee to the river and take refuge on an island. Although the battle continued for some time, an impasse was reached and the war—weary Indians finally returned to their respective villages. The Ojibwe claimed the Dakotas had suffered severe losses but admitted to losing eight warriors in addition to the three lost in the fire. Since the Ojibwe of that day were recognized as superior marksmen (they may have been using guns for more years than the Dakotas) it is entirely possible that the report is accurate.

The following year, Great Marten led a second campaign down the Mississippi. This time the war party was smaller in number — about sixty braves. At exactly the same spot where the Ojibwe had fought the Dakota Sioux the previous year, they again encountered a war party. But this time the invaders were seriously outnumbered — estimates ran as high as 400 Dakotas. Overnight, Great Marten's warriors dug in, taking time to dig fox holes up to three feet deep which would hold up to two men. The Dakota Sioux, meanwhile, had taken possession of a wooded area in range of the Ojibwe. Even though the Sioux completely outnumbered the Ojibwe, they were in no hurry to sacrifice their men with an open charge. Occasionally, a more daring brave would make a move and pay for it with his life. Then an equally brave (or foolish) enemy would dash out from cover to secure the scalp. Others would try to retrieve the body to prevent mutilation (which many believed could adversely effect the fallen brave's after-life). Hand to hand skirmishes resulted. On one such foray Great Marten — who had tempted death on scores of occasions over the years — lost his life. The Dakota Sioux had also suffered losses and that night retreated some distance. The Ojibwe, discouraged and saddened by the loss of their leader returned to their canoes under the shelter of darkness and headed for the north country.

The point of land between the Elk and Mississippi Rivers — where both battles were fought — was thereafter called "Me-gaud-e-win-ing" or "Battle Ground."

It is difficult to comprehend the dangers and uncertainties of living in the continent's heartland during this hundred year period. Not only was there open warfare with muskets — not just bows and arrows — but no village, no hunter, not even the women and children gathering wild rice or maple sap were safe from the marauding bands of Ojibwe and Dakota Sioux warriors.

How the Leech Lake Ojibwe Came to be Called "Pillagers"

Although this was not a battle between the Ojibwe and the Dakota Sioux, an incident at Pillager Creek (where it flows into the Crow Wing River) took place during the 100 years war and, as we shall see, had a devastating impact on nearly all the villages in Minnesota.

Because of the inter-tribal wars, few traders had ventured into the woodlands area for many years. In the spring of 1781, a trader, accompanied by a handful of voyageurs, traveled up the Mississippi. He chose the Crow Wing cut-off and camped at the mouth of what is now called Pillager Creek. Here he took ill and was forced to rest. A band of Leech Lake Ojibwe — perhaps out to make sure there were no Sioux war parties in the area, came across the sick trader and his men. Upon seeing his goods they were most anxious to do business; after all, for more than a generation they had been forced to travel to La Pointe, Grand Portage, Ontario, or Mackinac to do their trading. The trader, however, was too ill to do business. But the Indians were not to be denied. As the story goes, they at first intended to leave items of equal value to those taken, but when a cask of "firewater" was discovered and consumed, their judgment was clouded. As matters grew worse, the voyageurs placed the trader in his canoe and headed back down river. The next day, near the present site of Sauk Rapids, the trader died.

It is said that the Leech Lake band of Ojibwe received the name "Pillagers" because of the pillaging that took place here. Even other Indians called them "Muk-im-dua-Wine-Wug," which means to take by force. The city, the creek and the tribe all received their names from this incident.

When the news reached the Ojibwe leadership on Leech Lake, there was much consternation. Now, they feared, it would be many more years before a trader would again venture into their area. Thus it was, that the next year, 1782, a delegation was sent from Leech Lake to Mackinac – then a British fort – to make amends. Their peace offering of furs was well received and the English gave them in return a bale of goods, a British flag (assuming correctly, that the Indians had not yet learned the colonies had won the war), and a coat and medal for their chief. On their return trip, the happy Leech Lake delegation stopped at Fond du Lac and proudly displayed their goods. They may have been contaminated with smallpox germs. In a matter of days the village was all but wiped out by the dread disease – including the leader of the Leech Lake group. Survivors fled, carrying the disease with them to all parts of the lake region. According to legend, the British had instructed the Indians not to open their goods until they had arrived to their village. Some hold this as evidence that the English had planted contaminated goods; others say the instructions were given because the English had lost the Revolutionary War and by displaying the flag someone might inform the Indians of the outcome, thus making them less inclined to cooperate with the English. At any rate, the plague was spread by this incident. However, by the time the Leech lake Indians had returned to their villages, the disease had apparently run its course and the Leech area itself was not as severely affected as other villages.

It is also believed that smallpox entered Minnesota from the west. The carriers in this case were a party of Assiniboins, Cree and Ojibwe who had come upon a village in North Dakota – either Mandans or Gros Ventres –which was experiencing a smallpox devastation. There was little resistance and the war party took many scalps. When they returned to the boundary waters with their infected trophies they spread the disease across what it now northern Minnesota and into Ontario. Some historians believe this may have been the source of infection in Fond du Lac and that it arrived simultaneously with the Leech Lake Indians returning from Mackinac.

Whatever the source, the devastation was beyond present-day comprehension. The huge village at Sandy Lake was reduced to seven wigwams. Other villages were even less fortunate; sometimes there were no survivors. Jean Baptiste Cadotte, the French trader, sent this only slightly exaggerated message to Mackinac: "All the Indians from Fond du Lac, Rainy Lake, Sandy Lake and surrounding places are dead from smallpox."

But all did not die, and the villages were eventually repopulated.

Some of Flat Mouth's Raids On The Dakota Sioux

Although Flat Mouth was usually a man of peace, he not only defended the area against Dakota Sioux attacks, but participated in raiding parties to the west and south, almost always organized for reasons of revenge. These raids were often in alliance with tribes from other lakes. A frequent ally was Ba-be-sig-undi-bay or "Curly Head," the principal chief of the Gull Lake and Crow Wing Ojibwe. On one occasion, the two chiefs joined forces to avenge the deaths of Flat Mouth's nephew and two of Curly Head's allies: Waubo-o-jeeg (name-sake of the famous Wisconsin chief of the previous century) and She-shebe (hero of the Cross Lake massacre)[7]. Their joint forces nearly wiped out a Dakota Sioux village in the Long Prairie

Eshke-bog-e-coshe (Flat-Mouth) of Leech Lake. Bust by Francis Vincenti. Location: Senate wing, third floor, east. (One of only three Indian statues in the U.S. Capitol).

Courtesy of the Cass County Historical Society

area. A handful of Sioux prevented the Ojibwe from taking scalps, but Flat Mouth and Curly Head returned to their respective lakes with their desire for revenge satisfied. The Dakota Sioux never again attempted to establish a permanent village in the Long Prairie area.

In the spring of 1832, Flat Mouth led a party against the Dakota Sioux west of the Crow Wing River, possibly in the Wadena area. Three Dakotas were killed and another three wounded. He lost one of his own men; an ally from Cass Lake.

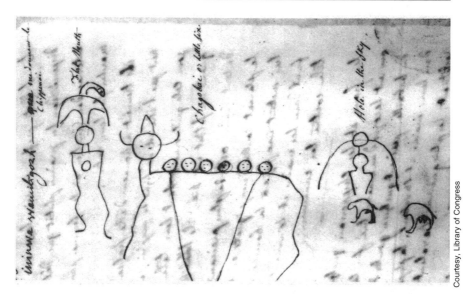

The pictorial signatures of three powerful Minnesota Chiefs: Flat Mouth, Shakopee and Hole-In-The-Day.

A younger Flat Mouth joined about 130 Red Lake warriors (some of them relatives of Uk-ke-waus) in avenging their deaths. He was on his way home from visiting his Cree relatives in the north and had stopped to hunt with friends at Red Lake. He later recalled that it was winter and they used snow shoes until they reached the windswept prairies to the west. He also told of impressive herds of buffalo along the way. Although it was preferred to take revenge against those who had killed your own people, satisfaction was often achieved by retaliating against whomever was available from that tribe. This was apparently the case here. The avengers came upon a Dakota Sioux village of about 50 lodges and fired volley after volley into the teepees. Heavy fire was returned and the small Ojibwe army retreated—satisfied that appropriate retaliation had been taken. Flat Mouth and two other warriors stayed behind, however, and approached the village once again under cover of darkness. They emptied their guns into a group of mourners and then escaped into the night.

Flat Mouth also told William Warren of his conquest of the Yankton–Sioux chief, Shappa. The story begins with Flat Mouth and his family camped on Otter Tail Lake at the outlet of Otter Tail Creek. Other members of the Leech Lake band were scattered throughout the area—hunting, trapping and collecting wild rice.

A huge Yankton Sioux war party (400 by Flat Mouth's estimates) passed through the area, moving in the direction of Battle Lake. Fortunately, they missed all Ojibwe camps except an outpost on a small

Courtesy Minnesota Historical Society

Waub-o-jeeg (White Fisher). White Cloud. Na-sho-tah (Twin)

Three generations of Ojibwe chiefs, father, son and grandson. At the top in the oval, is the war chief and ally of Chief Curly Head who was killed while ice fishing on Mille Lacs Lake; on the left is his son, White Cloud; and on the right is his grandson, an Episcopal priest who took the English name, Charles T. Wright. He served on Leech Lake.

unnamed lake where two of Flat Mouth's cousins were taking beaver. The two Pillagers fought bravely, killing three Sioux and wounding others. They were successful in retreating to a small rock outcropping on the lake, but were still in range of both guns and arrows from the shore. They quickly erected a rock wall. The Yankton Sioux, however, cut logs which they floated and pushed in front of them as they approached the islet. The

Pillagers finally ran out of ammunition and it was all over.

In examining the campsite the Yankton Sioux had used the night before, Flat Mouth found that four Yankton Chiefs had left their identification marks on trees, including the beaver image of Chief Shappa. After returning to Leech Lake, Flat Mouth sent his warpipe and warclub to neighboring villages, seeking to recruit an army of vengeance. Meanwhile, Shappa heard of the Ojibwe plans, probably through Col. Dickson who was married to his sister, and sent word to Flat Mouth through the Englishman that he had not been involved in the murder of his cousins and wanted to talk peace. He asked that there be a meeting at a trading post located on the Red River. Flat Mouth chose 30 of his best braves and set out for the powwow. When he arrived at the trading post, he found four Frenchmen in charge. The next day Shappa arrived with only two of his braves. Flat Mouth made it clear from the outset that he did not believe the Sioux Chief's claim of innocence and refused to smoke the peace pipe. Shappa knew he was doomed and spent the night praying and singing to the spirits. For some reason, Flat Mouth did not want to witness the bloodshed, so he asked his men to take the three Yankton Sioux out on the prairies, away from the Trading Post—so as not to involve the white men—and do what they wished with the captives. Flat Mouth did tell his men, however, that he would take responsibility for their deeds. The men did as told and after shooting the braves, cut off their heads.

Col. Dickson was naturally very upset by the death of his brother-in-law and told Flat Mouth that the trading posts on Leech Lake would be closed. It proved to be an idle threat, but was one more factor in the escalating enmity between the red-bearded trader and Chief Flat Mouth.

It is interesting that we have no record of Flat Mouth ever initiating any action against the Sioux; his acts of aggression were taken in retaliation.

Other Skirmishes

There were many other battles during the 100 years of fighting but they did not involve Leech Lake warriors[4], so they will not be described here. It is pretty safe to assume that there was a struggle for control of each of the major lakes in the Minnesota woodlands, from Mille Lacs Lake north.

It is interesting that during all of this fighting, very few whites were killed until the conflict in the New Ulm–Mankato area in 1862.[5]

In 1804 three traders were killed by the Ojibwe but they insisted they had mistaken them for Sioux Indians. Zebulon Pike, in his journal, made reference to "an American" killed by the Ojibwe at Red Lake in 1804. There may have been others.

Many whites reported close calls. For example, Chief Hole-in-the-Day (the younger) of Gull Lake in 1862 (at the same time as the white—Sioux conflict in Southern Minnesota) urged the Ojibwe to kill the whites living in northern Minnesota. He even burned the St. Colomba Mission on Gull Lake. Many whites were captured and brought to the narrows between Gull and Round Lakes. Others fled to Fort Ripley north of Little Falls. If it had not been for the intervention of Chiefs Big Dog and Buffalo of Leech Lake, Chief Bad Boy of Mille Lacs Lake, Father Pierz and a few other brave whites, there very likely would have been a large number of deaths. The Leech Lake chiefs warned Hole-in-the-Day that the white military would

Chief Hole-in-the-Day, the younger.

Courtesy of the Minnesota Historical Society

surely take revenge. Chief Bad Boy of Mille Lacs Lake sent word that he would protect the whites. Father Pierz pleaded for reason. Reluctantly, Hole-in-the-Day set his captives free.

In a possibly related incident, a Lutheran church on Mission Lake was also burned in 1862.

St. Colomba Church, Gull Lake, burned by Chief Hole-in-the-Day in 1862.

Courtesy of the Crow Wing County Historical Society

Courtesy of the Cass County Historical Society

When the Dakotas were pushed out of Minnesota by the military in 1862, the 100 yeas war came to an end. We will never know how much blood was shed or how many families were shattered during the more than a century of fighting. Sadly — as with most wars — it was for naught. From the original take over of the woodlands by the Ojibwe to the time of the Civil War, nothing really changed. The Dakota Sioux never regained one inch of their original woodland domain, nor did the Ojibwe capture any of the prairie country. Nothing was gained and a great deal was lost by both sides.

Chief Bad Boy of Mille Lacs Lake. He warned Chief Hole-in-the-Day that he would protect the white settlers.

[1]There was a belief held by some that a person who lost his scalp would appear that way in the hereafter.

[2]If they had come from the prairies farther west, (North Dakota), they would have been Nakotas rather than Dakotas.

[3]Warren, William, History of the Ojibways

[4]For further information, consult the book "The Indian Wars" by this author.

[5]Approximately 500 whites were killed and an unknown number of Dakotas. We do know that 38 Native Americans were hanged at the end of the conflict. For further information on this subject, consult "The Indian Wars" or "Our Historic Upper Mississippi" by this author.

Minnesota in 1852

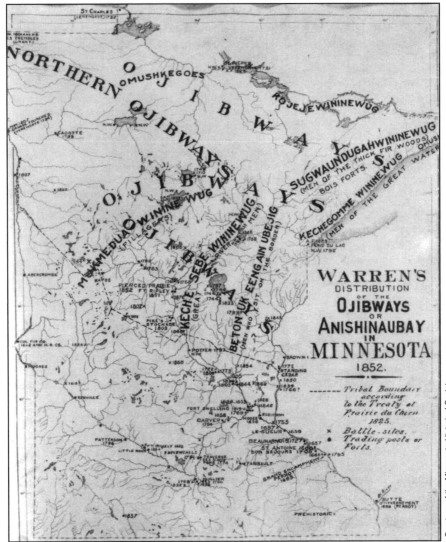

CHAPTER IV

Ojibwe Leaders

Unfortunately, we know nothing of the Sioux leadership during their tenure on Leech Lake in the 1600's and early 1700's. Since they were the ancestors of men like Little Crow; we can assume there was however, no lack of leadership. Neither oral or written history is of help. On the other hand, thanks to William Warren's "History of the Ojibways" and his extensive talks with Chief Flat Mouth and other Ojibwe leaders of that day, we have a very good record of the important chiefs during the Ojibwe rule of the lake. The white explorers, traders and missionaries who arrived in the late 1700's and in the 1800's further documented the Ojibwe leadership and history.

Among the chiefs who had prominent roles in driving the Sioux from the lake region of Minnesota but who were headquartered at nearby Sandy lake, were:

BI-AUS-WA, generally accepted as the leader of the first successful attacks on Sandy Lake. He was the principal chief of the Sandy Lake village during its first years as capital of the Ojibwe Nation. Bi-aus-wa was better known, however, for his civil leadership than as a war chief.

NOKA, a war chief who fought under Bi-aus-wa's leadership and for whom the Nokasippi was named. He was grandfather of the Waub-o-jeeg of the 19th century. Noka was a leader of the Ojibwe war party of 200 braves which wiped out a Sioux village near the mouth of the Minnesota River in retaliation for the destruction of the Sandy Lake village. When the Ojibwe left the north country the ice was just out and there were no leaves on the trees. They were surprised to find the trees in full leaf farther south and for that reason gave the name "Osh-ke-bug-e-sebe" or "New Leaf River" to the stream we now call the Minnesota River.

KECH-WA-BI-SHE-SHI, or "Great Marten," who when killed near Elk River was said to have fought in nearly 100 battles and been wounded in many of them. He was Bi-aus-wah's most important war chief and led every major compaign against the Sioux after the Ojibwe had settled in the northern region of Minnesota.

WAUB-O-JEEG I, or "White Fisher," the Ojibwe leader who not only drove the Sioux from the Wisconsin lake region (Battle of St. Croix Falls) but also the Sauk and the Fox — both Algonquin tribes which had allied themselves with the Dakota. He not only earned a reputation in Minnesota but also made the Minnesota invasion possible by securing northern Wisconsin for the Ojibwe.

Leech lake Leaders:

WAUS-E-KO-GUBIGS, or "Bright Forehead," grandfather of Flat Mouth, who was destined to become Leech Lake's most distinguished chieftain.

WA-SON-AUN-E-QUA, or "Yellow Hair," father of Flat Mouth. According to his illustrious son, Yellow Hair achieved his power through his knowledge of medicines and poisons. He hunted the area around Long Prairie, where he lost his oldest son in an attack by the Sioux. He gained revenge by killing and wounding several Dakotas and scalping alive a girl offered to him as a replacement for his own lost children.

UK-KE-WAUS, who was not really a chief but who led a reluctant band of forty-five Leech Lake warriors on a raid of Sioux villages in the Leaf Lakes and Battle Lake area. Uk-ke-waus and his sons were heroic in their deaths that made it possible for a remnant of the Ojibwe to escape the conquering Sioux.

ESHKE-BOG-E-COSHE, called "Gueule Platte" by the French traders and "Flat Mouth" by the English and Americans. Literally, the French words are translated: platte — meaning flat, and gueule — meaning the mouth of an animal. So the expression was hardly intended to be complimentary.

Born in the early 1700's, after the Sioux had been routed from their lake region strongholds, Flat Mouth's leadership came during a time when the major concern was holding Leech Lake against Dakota attacks. White explorers and traders quickly recognized him as the most influential chief of the lake.

Flat Mouth saw, and was part of, the years of historic development of our state. When the Pike Expedition reached Leech Lake in 1806, he was already a powerful chief. In 1812, when Col. Robert Dickson speaking for the British tried to persuade the Ojibwe to join them in their war against the United States, it was Flat Mouth who said "no" and whose leadership was a factor in keeping 99 percent of the Minnesota Ojibwe loyal to the American "Long Knives." In 1832, when Henry Schoolcraft visited Leech, Flat Mouth was older but no less powerful. When the time came for negotiations and treaties with the United States Government, it was Flat Mouth who represented the Leech Lake area Pillagers. Several times he was brought to Washington D.C., and on one occasion posed for the magnificent piece of sculpture still on display in the United States Capitol (one of only three Indians so honored). His life spanned our nation's formative years between the Revolution and the Civil War. Flat Mouth's village was located on Otter Tail Point by the north narrows. This was almost as easily defended as one of the islands.

As reported in the previous chapter, when necessary, Flat Mouth was a man of war. He not only defended his home base, but he participated in a number of raids against the Sioux. He joined with "Curly Head," the first great Ojibwe Chieftain at Gull Lake, in a raid on a Sioux Village near Long Prairie to avenge the death of his nephew and also of two popular Ojibwe leaders and warriors — Waub-o-jeeg II (namesake of the famous Wisconsin Chief of the previous century) and She-shebe (hero of the Cross Lake massacre of the Ojibwe by the Sioux). After nearly wiping out the entire village, a handful of brave Sioux kept Flat Mouth's warriors from taking scalps. The Dakotas moved out following this defeat and never again attempted to establish a permanent village in the Long Prairie area.[1] But mostly, Flat Mouth was a man of peace. Although loyal to the United States he grew uneasy and unhappy with white intrusions, yet, his contributions were many in the peaceful and orderly early development of the lake region of Minnesota.

Flat Mouth was, without a doubt, the most powerful Chief to reside on Leech Lake and was probably the most influential Ojibwe leader in the history of Minnesota. His name is found on all treaties effecting central and north central Minnesota between 1825 (the Treaty of Prairie du Chien) and his death in 1860. As already stated, he visited Washington D.C. several times and his statue remains in the United States Capital building. It is appropriate, therefore, to take considerable space here to report what the early white visitors had to say about him:

Rev. William Boutwell, Presbyterian missionary, gave this account of Flat Mouth in the "Boston Missionary Herald" in 1834: (He had visited Leech Lake with Henry Schoolcraft two years earlier and then returned as a missionary in 1833).

> . . . the principal chief (Flat Mouth) sent his "Mishinne," waiting-man, requesting Mr. Schoolcraft to come and breakfast with him.
>
> Decorum required him to comply with the request, though he was at liberty to furnish the table mostly himself. A mat spread in the middle of the floor served as a table, upon which the dishes were placed. Around this were spread others upon which the guests sat while the wife of the chief waited upon the table, and poured the tea. She afterward took breakfast by herself. After breakfast they proceeded to the Chief's headquarters which was thus described. "It is a building perhaps twenty feet by twenty-five, made of logs, which I

*am informed was presented to him by one of the traders. As we
entered, the old chief, bare-legged and bare-foot, sat with much dig-
nity upon a cassette. A blanket, and cloth about the loins, covered
his otherwise naked body, which was painted black. His chief men
occupied a bench by his side, while forty or more of his warriors sat
on the floor around the walls of his room smoking. The old man
arose and gave us his hand as we were introduced, bidding us to
take a seat at his right, on his bed. As I cast my eye around upon
his savage group, for once, I wished I possessed the painter's skill.
The old chief had again returned to his seat upon the large wooden
trunk, and as if to sit a little more like a white man than an Indian,
had thrown one leg across the other knee. His warriors were all
feathered, painted and equipped for service. Many of them wore the
insignia of courage, a strip of polecat skin around the head or
heels, the bushy tail of the latter so attached as to drag on the
ground; the crown of the head was ornamented with feathers, indicating the number of enemies the individual had killed, on one of
which I counted no less than twelve.*

*One side of his room was hung with an English and American
flag, medals, war-clubs, lances, tomahawks, arrows and other implements of death. The subject of vaccination was now presented to the
chief, with which he was pleased, and ordered his people to assem-
ble for that purpose. I stood by the doctor, and kept the minutes
while he performed the business.*

*Preparations were now made for taking our leave when the chief
arose, and giving his hand to each, spoke as follows, in reply to Mr.
Schoolcraft, who had addressed them as "My children." "You call us
children. We are not children but men. When I think of the condition of my people I can hardly refrain from tears. It is so melan-
choly that even the trees weep over it. When I heard that you were
coming to visit us, I felt inclined to go and meet you. I hoped that
you would bring us relief. But if you did not furnish some relief, I
thought I should go farther, to the people who wear big hats, in
hopes of obtaining that relief from them, which the Long Knives
(Americans) have so often promised.*

*Our great Father promised us, when we smoked the pipe with the
Sioux at Prairie du Chien in 1825, and at Fond du Lac in 1826,
that the first party who crossed the line, and broke the treaty,
should be punished. This promise has not been fulfilled. Not a year
has passed but some of our young men, our wives, and our children
have fallen, and the blood that has begun to flow will not soon stop.
I do not expect this year will close before more of my young men
will fall. When my son was killed, about a year since, I determined*

*not to lay down any arms as
long as I can see the light of the
sun. I do not think the Great
Spirit ever made us to sit still
and see our young men, our
wives and our children murdered."*

*"Since we have listened to the
Long Knives, we have not pros-
pered. They are not willing we
should go ourselves, and flog
our enemies, nor do they fulfill
their promise and do it for us."*

*The medals of each chief and
a string of wampum were now
brought forth stained with ver-
milion.*

*"See our medals," and hold-
ing them up the by strings, he
continued:*

**Chief Flat Mouth as he dressed for his
visits to Washington D.C.**

*"These and all your letters are stained with blood. I return them
all to you to make them bright. None of us wish to receive them
back," laying them at Mr. Schoolcraft's feet, "until you have wiped
off the blood."*

*Here a shout of approbation was raised by all his warriors pre-
sent, and the old man, growing more eloquent, forgot that he was
holding his blanket around his naked body with one hand, and it
dropped from about him, and he proceeded:*

*"The words of the Long Knives have passed through our forests
as a rushing wind, but they have been words merely. They have
only shaken the trees, but have not stopped to break them down,
nor even to make the rough places smooth."*

*"It is not that we wish to be at war with the Sioux, but when they
enter our country and kill our people, we are obliged to revenge
their death. Nor will I conceal from you the fact that I have already
sent tobacco and pipestems to different bands to invite them to come
to our relief. We have been successful in the late war, but we do not
feel that we have taken sufficient revenge."*

*Here a bundle of sticks two inches long was presented, indicating
the number of Ojibways killed by the Sioux since the treaty of 1825,
amounting to forty-three. Just as we were ready to embark, the old
man came out in his regimentals, a military coat faced with red,
ruffled shirt, hat, pantaloons, gloves and shoes. So entirely changed*

was his appearance that I did not recognize him until he spoke.

When Schoolcraft arrived at Leech (1832), he found an American Fur Company trading post located just east of Flat Mouth's village on Otter Tail Point. Some of the original Canadian traders were still on the lake (among them Rosseau) but operating under a license issued to John Fairbanks by the American Company. Aliens were not eligible for a license.

Boutwell returned to Leech Lake in 1833 and organized a Presbyterian mission school on Trader Bay. His diary tells of living in a wigwam and of great physical hardship.

LIEUTENANT JAMES ALLEN, who led the military escort for Schoolcraft, gave the following account:

July 17—The village of our encampment was Flat Mouth's...who is the principal chief of his band, and perhaps one of the most powerful and influential men of his whole nation. He is also their principal orator, and on all occasions like the present, when councils are held on their general interest, he is looked up to with great confidence and respect, and depended upon to say and do whatever is necessary for the benefit of the whole.

His (Flat Mouth's) manner was bold and vehement, particularly when he spoke of the Sioux; and, from the glow of excitement in the eyes and countenances of his warriors, I could see that they fully entered into his feeling.

They (the Pillagers) have several war chiefs who are much superior, in appearance, to Flat Mouth, and who have a much better character for warlike qualities. But the latter is the great chief in council, where his oratory sustains his authority; and he is acknowledged, by all, their principal chief.

DOUGLASS HOUGHTON left us this appraisal:

Their chief Flat Mouth has perhaps more absolute authority than any other of the Chippewa nation. He is a man of dignified commanding appearance and extremely ceremonious. We had before our arrival heard the traders say much of him; and his independence(s) and authority is a great annoyance to them.

SCHOOLCRAFT had this to add about Flat Mouth:

I was rather confirmed in the favorable opinions I have before expressed of him (Flat Mouth) and particularly in the ordinary, sober routine of his reflections and the habitual, easy manner, which he evidenced of arriving at correct conclusions.

....(Flat Mouth) is the ruler of the Pillager band, exercising the authority of both a civil and war chief. And he is endowed with talents which certainly entitle him to this distinction.

The chief brought me a letter from the interior some years ago, at St. Mary's, in which he is spoken of as "the most respectable man in the Chippewa country." And if the term was applied to his mental qualities, and the power of drawing just conclusions from known premises, and the effects, which these had on his standing and influence with his own band, it is not misapplied. Shrewdness and quickness most of the chiefs possess, but there is more of the character of common sense and practical reflection, in the Gueula Plat's remarks, than, with a very extensive acquaintance, I recollect to have noticed in most of the chiefs now living, of this tribe. He is both a warrior and a counselor, and these distinctions he holds, not from any hereditary right, for he is a self-made man, but from the force of his own character. I found him ready to converse on the topics of most interest to him. And the sentiments he uttered on the Sioux war, the fur trade, and the location of trading posts and agencies, were such as would occur to a mind which has possessed itself of the facts, and was capable of reasoning from them. His manners were grave and dignified, and his oratory such as to render him popular with his tribe.

The chief Aishkebuggekozh, himself, has a countenance of a very ogre. He is over six feet high, very brawny, and stout. That feature of his countenance from which he is named Flat Mouth, consisting of a broad expansion and protrusion of the front jaws, between the long incision of the mouth, reminds one much of a bull-dog's jaw.

KECHI OSAYE, or "Elder Brother," was a contemporary of Flat Mouth and considered an ally. Although he held the rank of chief and ruled over his own village, he was not as powerful as Flat Mouth and held a secondary position in the hierarchy. W.T. Boutwell, the Presbyterian missionary we quoted earlier, described Elder Brother as "An Indian among a thousand for his sincerity, integrity, and inflexible love of truth and equity. He is the most worthy Indian I have ever met...."

MAJI-GABO I, who as described by Henry Schoolcraft when he met him at Leech Lake in 1832, as "tall, gaunt and savage looking." The description fits his reputation well. In 1816, he participated in the "Seven Oaks Massacre" at Pembina and was "credited" with slaying and scalping Governor Robert Semple. When the foray was over, twenty-two settlers had been slain, scalped and their bodies mutilated. The action was an extension of the bloody feud between the Hudson's Bay Co. and the Northwest Co. Lord Selkirk, a Scotsman, had been granted domain over the upper Red River Valley area by the Hudson's Bay Co. He, in turn, had appointed Semple as Governor of the region with a fortified headquarters at Pembina. The massacre was regarded by Selkirk and the Hudson's Bay Co. as the work of the rival Northwest Company, which had been organized by Montreal merchants as a means of competing with the huge trading company.

John Tanner[2], the legendary 19th century hero of Lake of the Woods, earned a life-long stipend or pension from Lord Selkirk by leading a counterattack the following winter and recapturing the post in a daring night raid.

The rivalry between the two giant trading companies became so bloody they finally concluded everyone would eventually lose unless they joined forces. The merger occurred in 1821, and the new company was known thereafter and until this day as the Hudson's Bay Co.[3]

Chief Maji-gabo eventually settled at Leech Lake, where he became a close ally and "war chief" for Flat Mouth.

MAJI-GABO the younger, son of Majo-Gabo I, was chief of the Bear Island Pillagers at the time of the 1898 uprising and the formative years of the community of Walker. He was a brother of "Old Bug". In his later years he was a close friend of Mayor McGarry and a protector of whites living on the lake.

WA-BO-SE, or "Rabbit." We first hear of Wa-bo-se when he settled on the Mississippi near the mouth of Pine River. Rabbit Lake and later the Rabbit Lake reservation were named for him. Later he moved to Leech Lake and located on what is known to this day as Waboose Bay. He took as his wife the sister of Maji-gabo.

Maji-Gabo II. Chief of the Pillager Band of Ojibwe on Bear Island at the time of the 1898 uprising. Upon his death he willed everything he owned, including his title, 15 wives and children to Patrick McGarry, the first mayor of Walker.

Courtesy of the Cass County Historical Society

CHI-ANAQUOT, or Great Cloud, also a contemporary of Flat Mouth, but described as a leader of a different "faction" of Pillagers. There is no indication, however, that the division was serious; the Dakotas were too great a common enemy.

PE-ZHE-KE, or Buffalo, who was among those Leech Lake chieftains who inherited some of the prestige and power of Flat Mouth following his death. As stated earlier, in 1862, at the time of the great Sioux uprisings and massacres in southern Minnesota, the Ojibwe were planning an uprising of their own in northern Minnesota. Many believe there was an alliance between Little Crow – the legendary Dakota Chief – and Hole-in-the-Day of the Ojibwes.[4] The Leech Lake Pillagers were anxious to join in the Ojibwe

Pe-zhe-Ke or "Buffalo." His wisdom saved many white lives.

uprising and there is every reason to believe that if the younger braves had prevailed there would have been a great loss of life among the scattered white settlers of the Lake region. The Leech Indians were expected to join Hole-in-the-Day at the isthmus of land between Round and Gull Lakes (along with war parties from all over the lake area). Before leaving for the appointed rendezvous, zealous Leech Lake braves captured the handful of whites in the area and prepared to put them to death. Chief Buffalo and Chief Big Dog (who had also inherited some of Flat Mouth's influence) argued that it would be better to take them alive to Gull Lake just in case something had gone wrong with Hole-in-the-Day's plans and then they would be left "holding the bag" as murderers of white men. Fortunately, their logic prevailed.[5]

KECHI-ANI-MOS, or "Big Dog" as we have already indicated, was contemporary with Chief Buffalo and helped stop short a move to massacre whites in the area and then join with Chief Hole-in-the-Day in a general uprising which was to have originated at Gull Lake.

NEGONA-PIN-AY-SE, which means "Leading Bird," but who assumed the name of his deceased father and became Flat Mouth II. Although he inherited his father's mantle he earned the respect of his people in his own right and was of considerable influence among the Leech Lake Pillagers for the rest of the century.

KAY-GWAY-JAWAY-BENUNG, or Maji-gabo II, or "Red Blanket," who was the son of the original Maji-gabo, the renowned war chief of Flat Mouth's day. He was the Chief of the Bear Island Pillagers at the time of the historic 1898 Leech Lake uprising.

PUGONA-GESHIG, or "Hole-in-the-Day of Leech Lake," who was named "Old Bug"[6] by the whites. It was his refusal to submit to a subpoena that lead to the last Indian war in the United States, in 1898. We shall hear more of his story later. He was a brother of Red Blanket and son of Maji-gabo I.

KECHI-WAY-MITIG-OZBE, or "Great Frenchman." he was a half-brother to Chief Wa-bo-se and to Chief Mitig-gwah-kik-ens (Drum Beater) of Lake Pokegama. Great Frenchman was granted the title of "chief" by Flat

Courtesy of the Heartland Association

John Smith, son of Great Frenchman (Kechi-way-mitig-ozbe). He lived in the Leech Lake-Cass Lake area. He was born in the late 1700's and died in the 1900's, thus living in three centuries.

Mouth I because of the death of one of his sons at the hands of one of Flat Mouth's sons. He is best remembered as the father of John Smith, "the man who lived in three centuries[7]" — perhaps the oldest person to have ever lived in our state.

These last six leaders were in positions of influence when logging operations were begun on Leech Lake and the city of Walker was founded.

Nowhere among the Ojibwe peoples of the 18th and 19th centuries will we find greater leadership than on Leech Lake.

[1]A reservation for the Winnibago Sioux was later established at Long Prairie by the U.S. government.

[2]For additional information consult "White Indian Boy" and "Lake of the Woods, Yesterday and Today" by this author.

[3]For additional information consult "Lake Superior, Yesterday and Today" by this author.

[4]The two chiefs had been together at Fort Snelling just before the uprisings.

[5]For additional information, consult "The Indian Wars" by this author.

[6]In pronouncing Ojibwe names, the "P" is pronounced as a "B".

[7]Zapffe, Carl, "The Man Who Lived in Three Centuries".

CHAPTER V
Explorers, Traders and Missionaries

The first whites to visit the lake were French traders.[1] The French called the lake "Lac Gangsue," which would be translated "Bloodsucker Lake." It is believed that the Cree or Ojibwe originally gave the lake that name. When the English came along they chose to translate the name as Leech Lake, which sounds a little better than bloodsucker. The Sioux had earlier called it "White Bear" and Jonathan Carver identified it on his map drawn in 1760 as "White Deer Lake." Either would have been an improvement.

Nearly all books about North American history place great emphasis on who was the first whiteman[2] to discover "this place" or explore "that region." It is almost as though it doesn't matter that various Indian people have been in those places for nearly 8,000 years! As we pointed out earlier, white history is only about 5% of human history on this continent – including what is now Minnesota. But having said that, just who was the first Caucasian to look out upon our beloved Leech Lake?

The first recorded visit was by Louis La Verendrye, the youngest son of Pierre La Verendrye's four sons, in 1753. Louis La Verendrye was appointed commandant of LaPointe, on Madeline Island, Lake Superior, by the Governor General of Canada in 1752 for a three year term. His area of responsibility included the regions inhabited by the Ojibwe and Cree tribes in what is now Wisconsin and northern Minnesota. Meanwhile, another Frenchman, Paul Marin, was appointed (also by the Governor General) Commandant of the Upper Mississippi for the same term – essentially from Lake Pepin north to its source. At that time no one knew how far north the source was. The river probably was unexplored by whites very far north of present day Minneapolis. Maps of that day fairly accurately portrayed Lake Superior, Lake of the Woods and the lower Mississippi, because the French had been there. The Upper Mississippi, however, was drawn from descriptions by Native Americans and its source was shown north and west of Lake of the Woods. This fact, by the way, caused serious problems after the Revolutionary War when an effort was made to establish the border between the United States and Canada on the Lake of the Woods.

The regions of responsibility for La Verendrye and Marin overlapped when the Ojibwe and Cree took over the northern lakes area. It is because of this conflict of jurisdiction that we have a record of Louis La Verendrye's presence on Leech Lake in 1753.

Paul Marin was ordered to find the source of the Mississippi. To help in this endeavor he established a new fort about 100 miles north of Lake Pepin in 1752, which he called Fort Duquesne. The exact location of this fort is still in doubt, but at least three sites have been suggested: the mouth of the Crow Wing, the mouth of the Crow and a site north of Little Falls — all, of course, on the Mississippi. A man named Houl (first name probably Joseph) was placed in charge of the new fort. The next year, another voyageur, Paul Lacroix, was directed by Marin to lead a party of eight up the river in search of the headwaters.

Somewhere up the river (La Verendrye said it was about a day's journey south of Sandy Lake) on October 21, 1753, Lacroix encountered Louis La Verendrye and his party. It isn't hard to imagine the great surprise registered by both groups! La Verendrye accused Lacroix of trespassing in his domain. he told him that he had established a trading post on the Sunrise River at the headwaters of the Mississippi "near the Cree who reside on Bloodsucker (Leech) Lake." Because the Cree were La Verendrye's charge, he told Lacroix he was infringing. La Verendrye did not want competition, not even from his own countrymen. Since he had the rank of commandant and Lacroix was just a voyageur, La Verendrye placed all eight under arrest and escorted them back to Fort Duquesne. Here he told Houl to abandon the fort and move back farther south — which he did. La Verendrye confiscated all of the trade goods at the fort (and about 40 gallons of rum!) and returned to his post on the Sunrise River.

Houl wrote a letter of protest to his superior, Paul Marin, who had gone back east. This letter has been preserved and is a source of the above information. There is no record of how or if the issue was resolved. Actually, it mattered little since the British (as a result of the French and Indian War) were about to takeover the entire area anyway in 1763.

La Verendrye stayed on at Leech Lake for at least the 1753-54 trapping and trading season. We have no exact record of where La Verendrye's post was located. There has been speculation that the Sunrise River was the Leech Lake River, since the sun rises in the east and that river flows east out of Leech Lake. Because he said that it was near the Cree who lived on Leech Lake, it is safe to assume that La Verendrye was either on the lake or so close that he surely visited the lake several times.

The fact that La Verendrye did not encounter any of the Mississippi traders on his way to the Leech Lake area implies that he probably arrived there by way of Lake Superior, the St. Louis River and the Savanna Portage to Sandy Lake and the Mississippi.

It is interesting that the Sioux conflict with the Cree and Ojibwe had subsided enough at that time for traders to be on the upper Mississippi. It is significant that La Verendrye referred only to the Cree as being on Leech Lake at that time; this implies that the Ojibwe came later.

We stated earlier that Duluth visited the site that now bears his name in 1679 and that at that time he enlisted the help of the Ojibwe in trading with the Sioux. It is likely that these Ojibwe were the very first traders on the lake. The Ojibwe continued to trade for the French for about 60 years — up to 1739, after which hostilities broke out between the Sioux and the Cree, Assiniboin and — later — the Ojibwe.

Apart from La Verendrye, it is likely that white traders did not visit Leech lake until after the Ojibwe took over in 1766. In 1784, Alexander McKay lead an exploratory party from Montreal to Fond du Lac, on Lake Superior. Here, the party divided and one canoe, under the leadership of Jean Perrault,[3] traveled to the Mississippi and entered the lake through the Leech Lake River. It is believed he camped on Ottertail Point. Perrault returned in 1789 and established a winter post on Ottertail; Perrault, himself, wintered at Crow Wing (south of what is now Brainerd).

The Northwest Company established a post on Ottertail Point in 1796.

William Morrison was a trader on Leech Lake — starting in 1804. Hugh McGillis, also with the Northwest Company, was on the lake in the 1804-05 trading year.

Zebulon Pike further documented trading posts on Leech Lake when he visited there in 1806. Pike described a trading post with a stockade around it on Ottertail Point, "two miles from Flat Mouth's village at the north narrows of the point and across from Goose Island." At that time it was under the British Flag (although on American soil) and operated by the Northwest Company. Pike ordered the "Union Jack" shot down and replaced with the American Flag.

"Trader" Anderson operated a post on Oak (formerly "Squaw") Point at the time of Pike's visit. It is believed he worked for Colonel Robert Dickson, a British agent and independent trader. Dickson also had posts on Sandy Lake and the Mississippi.

Leech Lake was originally part of a territory claimed for France by Duluth, Perrot and others. A huge area north east of Leech Lake (including eastern Canada) was transferred to the British in 1763 after the French lost a series of battles and wars on this continent and elsewhere. The portion of this area south of the Canadian border was claimed by the United States after the Revolutionary War.

The area west of the Mississippi was part of the Louisiana Purchase (from France) in 1803 including Leech Lake.

We know that the Hudson's Bay Co. operated in the Canadian far north after it received its charter from the King of England in 1670, but it was their practice to let the Indians find their way to their posts on Hudson's Bay and other northern locations. Their traders did not reach out to the Indians in what is now southern Canada and northern United States until the competing Northwest Company[4] was formed and began making its way west in the early 1700's. That is when the La Verendryes and their French contemporaries established fortified trading posts on the Boundary Waters and points west.

In summary, the Ojibwe, as representatives of the French, were probably the first organized traders on Leech Lake (1679-1739). The French were the first to establish actual trading posts (as early as 1753 under Louis La Verendrye). The Northwest Company had at least two posts on Leech Lake. Even though many of the traders were French, they operated under the British flag (because they were on English soil). There were also independent traders on the lake. After 1806 — because of the outcome of the Revolutionary War and the Louisiana Purchase from France by the United States, all operations were (or were supposed to be) under the American flag.

There are records of most of the trading posts that were established in Minnesota and references are made to posts on Leech Lake at these locations:

FIVE MILE POINT . . . .*Northwest Company; later*
(5 miles south of the mouth of the Leech Lake River)   *American Fur Company*

OTTERTAIL POINT (southern tip) . . . .*Northwest Company; later*
                                                    American Fur Company

PINE POINT . . . .*Independent traders; later*
                                                    American Fur Company

OAK (formerly Squaw) POINT . . . .*Independent traders*

One mile south of LEECH LAKE RIVER OUTLET . . . .*Independent traders*

Bottom of TRADERS BAY . . . .*Independent traders; later*
                                                    American Fur Company

After the War of 1812, the American Fur Company was given ownership of all British posts south of the Canadian border, including, of course, Leech Lake.

We have good documentation of visits to Leech Lake by several explorers and missionaries in the 1800's, as follows:

LIEUTENANT ZEBULON PIKE

In 1805, Pike journeyed up the Mississippi in search of the source of the river. He was formally commissioned by General James Wilkinson (sometimes suspected of treasonous intent because of his friendship with Aaron Burr) to explore and take possession of the country and to gain permission from the Indians to construct a military fort and trading houses at strategic locations. Pike's subsequent negotiations with the Sioux were particularly significant in Minnesota history because Fort Snelling was later constructed on property secured as a result of the agreement reached with the Dakota Sioux.

The United States Government was aware of the fact that the British operated Northwest Company was still trading in the area. One of Pike's assignments was to advise the chief traders of these posts that duty must be paid on goods brought into our country (at Mackinac) and that they could no longer fly the British flag. In early winter Pike proceeded up the river but was forced to call a halt because of icing conditions on the Mississippi — about thirty miles south of its confluence with the Crow Wing (Pike Rapids).

Courtesy of the National Archives

Later that winter he proceeded, with his company of soldiers, to Leech Lake. The winter was apparently at first quite mild because the river ice proved unsafe. Much of the journey had to be overland; even so, sleds broke through ice on more than one occasion. Powder that was not stored in water-proof kegs had to

Lt. Zebulon Pike visited Leech Lake in 1806

be dried. The men barely escaped serious injury or death when the powder, being dried in iron kettles near a fire, blew up! At one point Pike's tent caught on fire and the powder stored there had to be hastily removed. Extreme cold set in, followed by nearly three feet of snow, and the troops were forced to stop about every three miles to build fires. In spite of all the hardships, the Northwest post at Sandy lake was finally reached; after a rest, they continued on to Leech Lake.

At Leech, he found a Northwest Company trading post, surrounded by a stockade, and located on Ottertail Point, two miles from Flat Mouth's village and across from Goose Island. This post was also under English control and the chiefs of the area were proud possessors of British flags and medals. Although cordially received and feasted with baked beaver and boiled moose head, Lt. Pike ordered the British flag shot down and replaced it with the stars and stripes. In a ceremony of February 16, 1806, he claimed the area in the name of the United States government. The Indians placed great significance on the occasion and exchanged their medals and flags for those of the United States. Flat Mouth, who was present at the ceremony, observed that on that day he "ceased to be an Englishman and became a Long Knife" (as the Indians referred to the Americans).

Pike was fully aware of the Ojibwe-Sioux hostilities and did his best to establish peace in the region. In his opening speech at Leech Lake he said, "I was chosen to ascend the Mississippi to bear to his red children the words of their father, and the Great Spirit has opened the eyes and ears of all the nations to listen to my words. The Sauks and Reynards are planting corn and raising cattle. The Winnebagos continue peaceable as usual, and even the Sioux have laid by the hatchet at my request. Yes, my brothers, the Sioux who have so long and obstinately warred against the Chippeways,[5] have agreed to lay by the hatchet, smoke the calumet, and again become your brothers. Brothers! You behold the pipe of Wabasha as a proof of what I say. The Little Corbeau, Fils de Pinchon and L'Aile Roughe, had marched two hundred and fifty warriors to revenge the blood of their women and children, slain last year at the St. Peters.[6] I sent a runner after them, stopped their march, and met them in council at the mouth of the St. Peters, where they promised to remain peaceable until my return; and if the Ouchipawan[5] chiefs accompanied me, to receive them as brothers, and accompany us to St. Louis, there to bury the hatchet, and smoke the pipe in the presence of our great war-chief; and to request him to punish those who first broke the peace...Brothers! I understand that one of your young men killed an American at Red Lake last year, but that the murderer is far off; let him keep so; send him where we may never hear of him more, for were he here I would be obliged to demand him of you, and make my young men shoot him."

A Red Lake Indian Chief "Old Sweet" was present, and responded thus, "My father! I have heard and understood the words of our great father. It overjoys me to see you make peace among us. I should have accompanied you had my family been present, and would have gone to see their father, the great war-chief.

"The medal I hold in my hand I received from the English chiefs. I willingly deliver it up to you. Wabasha's calumet with which I am presented, I receive with all my heart. Be assured that I will use my best endeavors to keep my young men quiet. There is my calumet, I send it to my father the great war-chief. What does it signify that I should go to see him?

"My father! you will meet the Sioux on your return. You may make them smoke in my pipe, and tell them that I have let fall my hatchet.

"My father! tell the Sioux on the upper part of the St. Peters River,[6] that they mark trees with the figure of a calumet, that we of Red Lake who go that way, should we see them, may make peace with them, being assured of their pacific disposition, when we shall see the calumet marked on the trees."

Flat Mouth gave similar assurances and designated his brother, Beau, and another chief called "The Buck" as personal emissaries to travel with Pike to visit the Sioux and then go on to St. Louis.

Pike was eventually promoted to brigadier general and died a hero's death in the war of 1812. Pike's peak in Colorado and Pike Bay of Cass Lake honor his name.

British Agents Invite The Pillagers To Join Them In The War of 1812

Although several Canadian Ojibwe tribes aligned themselves with the British in the War of 1812, virtually none of the Minnesota Ojibwe joined the English. However, every effort was made by the British to recruit the Minnesota Indians. Col. Robert Dickson, who had made a career of trading with the Dakotas and the northern Ojibwe, was perhaps the best known of the British agents who tried to persuade the Indians to fight against the Americans. He sent an interpreter by the name of St. Germain to Leech Lake to deliver presents and wampum belts to Flat Mouth as the most influential chief. A public meeting was held and Flat Mouth said (in later years to William Warren) that he had responded thus," When I go to war against my enemies, I do not call on the whites to join my warriors. The white people have quarreled among themselves, and I do not wish to meddle in their quarrels, nor do I intend ever, even to be guilty of breaking the windowglass of a white man's dwelling."

Wabasha, a hereditary Sioux Chief joined forces with Dickson; so did Joseph Renville — a Sioux half-breed and noted guide and interpreter who had served with Pike. Dickson and his Indian allies captured Mackinac without a shot, also Fort Shelby at Prairie du Chien. It is believed that many other Sioux warriors would have joined the British but were afraid the Ojibwe would attack their villages in their absence. It is likely that if Flat Mouth had brought the Pillagers to support the British, the Eastern States would have been in even greater difficulty than they were because of an attack from the West.

Henry Schoolcraft — 1820 and 1832

Schoolcraft had been chosen by Governor Lewis Cass (of the Michigan Territory) as a member of his 1820 expedition up the Mississippi for the following purposes as he had set them forth in a letter to Secretary of War Calhoun; "with a view to examine the production of its animal, vegetable and mineral kingdoms, to explore its facilities for water communication, to delineate its natural objects, and to ascertain its present and future probable value...." At that time, Schoolcraft was known as an author and mineralogist. The 1820's expedition apparently terminated at a lake Pike had called "Upper Red Cedar;" Schoolcraft renamed it "Cassina," in honor of the Governor. Today we call it "Cass Lake," and the lower lake we have named "Pike Bay."

In 1832, Schoolcraft was an Indian Agent, and he organized his own expedition. As we know, he successfully identified Lake Itasca as the true source of the Mississippi River. Late on July 16th, accompanied by an escort of soldiers (under the command of Lt. James Allen) and Rev. William T. Boutwell (a Presbyterian missionary who was then stationed at Mackinac) Schoolcraft arrived at Leech Lake.

When Schoolcraft arrived at Leech, he found an American Fur Company trading post located just east of Flat Mouth's village on Ottertail Point (likely the same post visited by Pike 26 years earlier). Some of the original Canadian traders were still on the lake (among them Rosseau) but operating under a license issued to John Fairbanks by the American Company. Aliens were not eligible for a license.

As Indian Agent, Schoolcraft was headquartered at Sault St. Marie. The Upper Mississippi was included in his jurisdiction. One of his assignments after the International Boundary was clearly established was to recommend sites for trading posts on the American side.

Reverend William T. Boutwell

We have already told of how Boutwell accompanied Schoolcraft on his second voyage up the Mississippi (1832) when he discovered the true source of the river, and Boutwell took credit for assisting him in creating a name for the lake (Itasca). We also quoted Boutwell's description of Chief Flat Mouth and his notes on the conversation between the chief and Schoolcraft. The missionary returned to Leech Lake the following year (1833) and established a Presbyterian mission school on First Point.[7] He was highly respected by the Indians and saved more than one white man from harassment—or worse—at the hands of the Pillagers, including Jospeh Nicollet. His diary tells of living in a wigwam and enduring great physical hardships. He left the lake in 1837.

Other Missionary Efforts:

Oberlin college missionaries occupied the Boutwell mission from 1843-1846.

An Episcopal missionary, the Rev. J.A. Gilfillan, was also on the lake; likewise a Native American Episcopal priest, Charles Wright. (see page 52)

Joseph Nicollet

In 1839, Nicollet set out to explore Lake Itasca and the surrounding area. He was a Frenchman and had been trained as a mathematician. He liked to work alone and often packed his equipment, which was considerable, across country on his back—including a thermometer, sextant, barometer, chronometer, compass, tape line, spyglass, gun, powder and shot. He did a good job of documenting the area.

He stopped on Leech Lake for one week in August on his way north, and again for a week on his way back in September. He spent considerable time with Boutwell and held extensive interviews with Chief Flat Mouth. Nicollet constructed a map of Leech Lake and named Pickering Bay after John Pickering of Massachusetts in appreciation for his work with Indian languages.

At the outset, some of the Indians threatened to deprive him of all his goods and, perhaps, would have had it not been for the intervention of Boutwell.

In 1838, the U.S. Government commissioned Nicollet to study the area between the Missouri and the Mississippi. Lt. John Freemont was his assistant. Their work produced the first reliable map of the West.

John Jacob Astor

Astor founded the American Fur Company in 1808, and made it a viable competitor to the Hudson's Bay Company and the Northwest Company. After the Canadian-United States border was established in 1821, he had a virtual monopoly of the fur trading business south of the border. Because the American government at that time would not allow the trading of liquor for furs, the A.F.C. operated at a significant disadvantage close to the border. The company had numerous posts on the Upper Mississippi and its tributaries. Shortly after the War of 1812, they moved in on the Northwest operations on Sandy, Leech and the Red Lakes.

In 1823, Astor sold out his interests in the company to Ramsay Crooks, his business associate, and turned to the east coast to further develop his financial operations.

Although it is likely he visited his posts on Leech Lake we could find no written record.

[1]If whites were, indeed, assimilated by the Mandan Indians, then they possibly passed this way and would have preceded the French.

[2]It is true that all early explorers were men.

[3]Perrault was clerk of the McKay expedition.

[4]The Northwest Company merged with its rival, the Hudson's Bay Company, in 1821. By that time, however, the Leech Lake posts were under the control of the American Fur Company.

[5]Another name for Ojibwe.

[6]The original name the whites gave to the Minnesota River.

[7]There is some confusion as to the location of Boutwell's mission. It is also reported as being on Trader Bay and Uran Bay. It is possible he used different sites at different times.

CHAPTER VI
The Last Indian War

If we were to ask someone from one of the eastern seaboard states where the last Military-Indian battle took place in our country – few would guess "Minnesota." But it is really not so surprising when we realize that northern Minnesota was about as underdeveloped in 1898 as any of the states of the West or Southwest.

The incident which brought troops to Leech Lake was in itself quite insignificant, and if a rifle had not fallen from its stacked position and accidentally discharged, there may have been no battle at all. However, the general discontent and restlessness of the Indians at that time made the incident possible. One might also speculate that the danger of a general Indian uprising across the lake region would have been much more likely except for the knowledge all Ojibwe had of how the Sioux had been literally driven out of southern Minnesota fifteen years earlier following the fighting which had taken place in the New Ulm–Mankato area.

The center of the controversy was Chief Pugona-geshig, called "Old Bug" by the whites. At the root of the problem was the illegal sale of liquor to the Indians. Government agents were seeking witnesses to convict "bootleggers" and "Old Bug" was being sought as such a witness for a trial which was to be held in Duluth. In his younger days, the chief had been taken to this same city for a similar procedure and was allegedly left to find his own way back to Leech Lake. As the story goes, he was twice thrown off trains for lack of a ticket. It was winter, and he endured many hardships, including freezing, before returning to his home on Leech Lake. He vowed never again to be subjected to such treatment and this time he hid in the forest. Eventually he was forced to come out of hiding to report at the old agency in Trader Bay in order to collect his regular census payment. He simply could not forego what he thought was rightfully his. U.S. Marshals promptly arrested him; when he resisted, he was handcuffed. At first, other Indians were hesitant to interfere, but his cries for help and taunting words finally shamed some of the younger braves into attacking the marshals and roughing them up. "Old Bug" made for the woods, but handicapped by his age and the shackles, he was caught again. This time a group of Indian women got into the act and the chief made good his escape. In the days that followed, a large number of Indians (particularly those on Bear Island where his brother, Maji-gabo was chief) rallied to his support and the marshals, recognizing their own limitations and the gravity of the situation, requested military support.

Law and order had to be maintained and a contingent of soldiers was

Chief Pugona-geshig (on the left), nicknamed "Old Bug" (the Ojibwe "P" is pronounced "B"). He was the focal point of the last U.S. Military-Indian war in our country. He was the son of Maji-gabo I (a war chief) and a brother of Red Blanket (Maji-gabo II).

Troops arrive in Walker, October, 1898

A cabin and garden belonging to "Old Chief Bug"–the setting for the last Indian–white war.

sent north under the leadership of General John Bacon and Major Melville C. Wilkinson. The author's father, Richard Lund, was living in Brainerd at the time; although only eight years old, he had vivid recollections of the troop trains as they pulled into that city on their way to Walker. Even though local citizens were apprehensive, they generally made light of the situation and cheered the soldiers on their way. He also recalled the some-what relieved but very sober crowd that greeted a returning train with its dead and wounded.

The first troop train arrived in September, the second just after the first of October, and a third came later. On the morning of October 5, 1898, General Bacon, Major Wilkinson and about two hundred soldiers set out from Walker on barges, headed for Sugar Point (now also called Battle Point) where the fugitive had his cabin home and a garden. The soldiers spent the morning searching in vain; they encountered only a few women and children. At noon, a group of men were instructed to break for lunch in a clearing by the log cabin. As they stacked their rifles, one fell and accidentally discharged. Unknown to the soldiers, there were scores of Indians hiding in the woods around the clearing. One or more of the Indians apparently assumed they had been discovered and returned fire. The soldiers took refuge in the cabin and continued the battle. By the time the Indians retreated into the oblivion of the forest, six soldiers lay dead, including Major Wilkinson (for whom the tiny village near Leech Lake on Highway 371 is named), and ten were wounded. The Indians apparently suffered no casualties although it was rumored that one had been killed. It is to the credit of the military that vengeance was not taken. "Old Bug" was allowed to make good his escape to the cabin of his broth-er, Chief Red Blanket, on Boy River, and peace was restored. When the citizens of the tiny village of Walker heard the shots from Sugar Point and when no one returned from the fighting to report its outcome, they feared the worst and assumed that the Indians had wiped out the military expe-dition. They called the Mayor of Brainerd and asked that he organize what amounted to a citizen's militia to help them. Mayor Nevers responded and a special train left Brainerd for Walker. Dr. James Camp[1] was among those who volunteered.

Pauline Wold,[2] who worked for Dr. Camp, wrote the following account of Brainerd's reaction to the uprising:

Leech lake was only sixty miles away, and Indians on the warpath might easily reach us! And with all our men and guns gone, we felt very much like "babes in the woods."

Few people in Brainerd slept much that night. The next day we tried to get into communication with Walker, but the wires had evi-dently been cut, and no trains were running. The second day wild rumors were abroad that Indians on their ponies had rushed

Courtesy of the Cass County Historical Society

The Steamer Flora pushes a barge filled with U.S. soldiers past the Lake View Hotel on Leech Lake toward the last battleground between American Indians and the U.S. Army.

Courtesy of the Cass County Historical Society

Soldiers of the United States Army, freshly returned from battlefields of the Spanish-American War, report for duty at City Dock in Walker.

*through town, but there was no news from Walker. On the morning
of the third day Mrs. Nevers[3] called to find out if we had heard anything at the hospital, but we had not. She said she had heard that
there had been a battle and that several men from Brainerd had
been injured or killed, among them, Dr. Camp. Not very good news
for us! We were all feeling pretty "jittery." On the following morning
a wire reached the hospital asking us to meet a train coming down
that morning, and to bring soup, hot coffee and surgical dressings. I
must admit we were rather an excited crowd at the station. With
sinking hearts we noticed as the train pulled in that there were several rough pine boxes in the baggage car. A shudder went through
me when I thought that perhaps Dr. Camp was in one of them!
Imagine our relief when the first to get off the train were Dr. Camp
and Mayor Nevers. The told us at once that all the men from
Brainerd were safe.*

*Not many questions were asked, as soon we were busy feeding
and dressing wounded soldiers and trying to make them a little
more comfortable for a trip down to Fort Snelling hospital. They
told us that half a dozen soldiers had been killed, among them the
beloved Major Melville C. Wilkinson, and that ten had been wounded. One of the boys had been shot through the thigh. They were
indignant to think that some of them had gone through the Cuban
campaign without a scratch, and here they were being killed by a
handful of Indians.*

*That evening we had a little party to welcome Dr. Camp. A few
neighbors came in, and we then heard from him what had really
happened. Upon reaching Walker, the Brainerd men found everything in great commotion and everyone scared to death. They heard
that the soldiers, eighty of them under the command of General
John M. Bacon and Major Wilkinson, had gone to Sugar Point near
Bear Island in the morning, as news had reached them that 'Old
Bug' had been seen there. At Walker a lot of shooting had been
heard during the day, but no one had returned to tell what was happening. It was feared that the Indians were getting the best of it.*

*As Dr. Camp had spent a couple of years as the resident physi-
cian at Fort Totten, the men elected him their leader, thinking that
perhaps he knew more about handling Indians than they did. So
the first thing he did was to gather all the women and children into
the Walker Hotel, the only brick building in town. Next he placed
guards on all the roads leading into town. 'I knew this was a very
foolish precaution,' said Dr. Camp, 'for if the Indians wanted to
come they would use their own trails that nobody else knew, and
they would not use the beaten highways. But I did this to let people*

Flat Mouth II in native and diplomatic dress.
Ogema Negona pin ay se or Chief Leading Bird, called Flat Mouth II by the Whites,
successor to his father Eske bog e coshe and Chief of the Ma Kun Dwe or Pillager
Ojibwe until his death July 24, 1907. Respected by Indians and whites alike, he
was a frequent visitor to our National Capital. By staying neutral, he helped prevent
an escalation of the 1898 conflict.

This is believed to be the first photograph of the village of Walker—taken about 1896.

Courtesy of the Minnesota Historical Society

The village of Cass Lake was worried, too. This fortification was still standing two or three years after the battle when this picture was taken.

know that something was being done. I thought it might act as a nerve sedative — something they needed very badly just then.'

The Brainerd group talked things over during the night and decided to cross the lake as soon as daybreak came and find out what was happening. Early the next morning they got a large barge and also some cordwood, which they piled in the center as a barricade to hide behind in case of need.

At the 'Narrows' before entering the big lake, the party found a band of Indians, headed by Chief Flat Mouth.[4] They called and asked, 'Where are you going?' The men answered. 'Over to Sugar Point to see what is happening over there,' and the Indians replied, 'We will be here when you come back.'

When the barge neared the point, the men went ahead very cautiously, not knowing what might be coming. Everything seemed very quiet, with only a few men running down to the beach. They seemed to be in soldiers uniforms, but that could be a disguise and they might be Indians. The newcomers beached their boat very carefully and went behind the barricade in case they should be shot at. To their relief however, they were greeted by soldiers and a couple of newspaper reporters who had gone along to write up the happenings at Leech Lake. A couple of more frightened men were never seen. They climbed aboard like two little monkeys and swiftly hid behind the barricade.'

Of course, by this time the action was over and the reporters had nothing to fear."

A slightly different version[5] of the conflict was reported in the August 6 edition of the Cass County Pioneer. It was written during the fighting.

INDIAN TROUBLE

War is now Raging with the Bear Island Indians.
6 Killed 12 Wounded.
Major Wilkinson Shot Thro' the Heart.
Town under Guard

200 Troops Just Arrived.

The Bear Island Indians are on the war path. Last night excitement ran high in Walker. The steamboats returning from the big lake brought news of a fierce battle between the Indians and the U.S. troops. The presence of wounded men and the holes made in the sides of the boats by rifle bullets from Indians guns, showed that the opposing forces had had a fierce engagement.

For some time trouble has been brewing on the reservation. The Indians have many grievances, the chief of which is with regard to the regulations of dead and down timber. About three weeks ago, two Indians arrested by U.S. deputy marshals were rescued by their comrades. The marshals determined to make the arrests and asked for troops. Twenty men were sent up but they were too few to accomplish anything. More troops were telegraphed for. Meanwhile, the Indians were preparing for war and bought up all the ammunition in Walker. They also left the Island and camped on the main land so that their retreat could not be cut off.

On Tuesday night 85 more troops arrived in town. Yesterday morning they took the steamers Flora, Chief and Jennie and steamed up the lake to Sugar Point where the Indians had congregated. The troops landed at 9 a.m. without opposition. At 11 two of the 22 Indians for whose arrest warrants were issued, were captured without a single shot being fired. The soldiers were standing in a group around the prisoners, when suddenly the crack of many rifles was heard. The Indians in the bush were firing upon the soldiers. The latter dropped to the ground and crawled to the bank of the lake for shelter. The Indians then fired at the three steamboats. On the Jennie, Pilot Joe Oscar was shot through the right arm. On the Flora, Ed Harris had his left arm shattered with a rifle ball. On the Chief, Engineer Howard Anway had a narrow escape, a ball passing through his sweater, while two bullets whistled through the pilot house in which was Inspector Tinker, who was slightly wounded.

The three boats then left the scene of combat and steamed back to Walker.

Meanwhile the soldiers, protected by the bank of the lake, began firing at the Indians and succeeded in driving them back. Several soldiers and Indians were killed, as reported by friendly Indians who left the battle field after the first fight. When the boats left, there were already quite a number of soldiers wounded. Immediately upon the return of the boats more troops were sent for, and 200 are expected at 2 p.m. today.

At seven o'clock last evening a false report was spread that the Indians had cut the telegraph wires. This looked as if they meant business. The citizens at once held a meeting in the town hall to organize a town guard. Mayor Kinkele presided. A line of pickets was placed around the town. All the citizens turned out with their rifles. The pickets were relieved by new volunteers every three hours. The Walker citizens were aided by twenty-five men from Brainerd who came up at 12 p.m. on a special train with 50 rifles and a large supply of cartridges. At 2 o'clock this morning a special train left Walker for Brainerd to meet the soldiers who are coming from St. Paul.

At 8 o'clock this morning the Flora left Walker with 30 volunteers and hospital supplies for the wounded.

U.S. Marshall O'Connor is doing the Shafter act and is running the Bear Island campaign from his cozy quarters in the Pameda Hotel.

Later – 9:30 a.m. Wm. Bonga, an Indian Interpreter has just come from the agency, up on the Zella. He reports that last night a Bear Island Indian runner arrived at the agency with the report that at the first fighting yesterday at noon, six soldiers were killed and four wounded. There was firing last night, but the result is as yet unknown.

Still Later – 11:45 a.m. The Vera has just arrived at the dock in Walker, from the scene of battle. On board are U.S. Deputy Marshal Tallman and one wounded soldier. To a Cass County PIONEER reporter M. Tallman said: "So far 5 are killed and 8 seriously wounded in addition to one Indian Police killed. The 5 whites killed are Major Wilkinson, a sergeant and 3 privates. We tried to put the wounded on board the Vera but the Indians opened fire on us so that we were able to take only one wounded with us. Our boys are entrenched not far from shore. The battle was waging when we left. There are about 60 Indians armed with Winchesters."

It was rumored last night that marshal Ed Warren and our popular barber Frank Briggs were both killed but Mr. Tallman says "neither of them are hurt, Briggs is fighting like a tiger,"

Although this was a serious conflict and blood was shed, it is important to note that the actual fighting was between the military and the Ojibwe; the white residents of the lake were not involved in the fighting. The relationships between the whites and the Ojibwes were actually quite good. We shall see in a later chapter, for example, how a leading chief, Maji-gabo II, when he died left everything he owned (including his wives and children) to Patrick McGarry, the white mayor of Walker.

[1]Dr. Camp was a highly respected and well-liked physician in Brainerd. He also owned a cabin near the thoroughfare between the Upper and Lower Mission Lakes. A "pothole" between the lakes and the Mississippi River is named for him. The author's father recalled that the doctor's well-trained horse would allow Camp to shoot partridges and other game from the buggy and would patiently wait while he retrieved them or gave chase.

[2]Wold, Pauline, Some recollections of the Leech Lake Uprising, Minnesota History, 1943.

[3]The wife of the Mayor of Brainerd.

[4]Chief Flat Mouth the younger. Although not as famous as his father he was highly respected by both whites and Native Americans. Edith Kulander, (a relative of the author) formerly of Walker, remembers Flat Mouth giving her mother his knife, with this assurance, "If any Indians ever bother you, show him my knife and he will leave you alone."

[5]It is the author's observation that it is not unusual for eye witnesses to give quite different reports of the same incident. We must also remember this article was written during the "heat of battle."

CHAPTER VII

Logging

There had been extensive logging in Minnesota for nearly 50 years before operations reached far enough north to include Leech Lake. The industry had its Minnesota beginnings in the triangle formed by the St. Croix and Mississippi Rivers, shortly after the signing of the Indian treaty of 1837.[1] Stillwater was the headquarters city, but those early logging operations reached as far north as Mille Lacs Lake. By 1847, ten years later, there was logging on the Crow Wing River. It was not until the early 1880's however, that the first trees were harvested around Leech Lake. T.B. Walker began purchasing land in 1882 and drove logs down the Leech Lake River in 1884. The Brainerd Lumber Co., however, actually felled the first trees. The city of Walker was not founded until 1896, with the coming of the railroad from Brainerd.

The lumber industry in the Leech Lake area is synonymous with the name of Thomas Barlow Walker — whose name is preserved through the community on the shores of Leech Lake and the Walker Art Gallery of Minneapolis. Born in Xenia, Ohio, in 1840, young Walker came to Minneapolis at twenty-two years of age. At nineteen, he had contracted for railroad ties at Paris, Illinois; next, he tried teaching; his first employment in Minnesota was as a surveyor for the St. Paul and Duluth Railroads. By 1868 he was owner of an extensive acreage of pine forests. One of his early mills was at Crookston.

In his years at Walker and in the Leech Lake area he was associated with a number of lumbermen, but the most significant of these associations was with Henry Akeley. For him he named the townsite where he constructed one of his largest mills when he became disgusted with the number of saloons in Walker. There was much consternation among the Walker businessmen when he announced his decision to build his new mill ten miles to the west; after all, they had named their new town after him in the hope he would build his mill there, but he could not be dissuaded. The original deeds for property in Akeley included the prohibition

Treaties Between
Minnesota Indian Tribes and
The United States Government[1]

[1]Red Lake Reserv not shown.

of liquor traffic. The Akeley of today is much smaller than the original lumbering "boom town."

The upper reaches of the Crow Wing and several of the lakes through which the river winds were logged-off by Walker and Akeley and in 1889 the partnership constructed a mill in that area.

Although Walker was by far the largest operator and he owned most of the land, there were others. First on the lake was the Brainerd Lumber Company, headed by a man named Cooke. The Leech Lake Lumber Co. and the Northland Pine Co. had sawmills at Walker. Weyerhauser was on the lake after 1904. The J. Neils Co. was also here.

T.B. Walker called his operation the Red River Lumber Co.; that was where he had begun logging. Maybe it was because the Walker company was the largest or maybe it was because they threw their weight around, but they were not liked by their competitors or some of the "locals."

Much of the region could not be harvested effectively without railroads; therefore it was logging that provided the original impetus for the construction of a network of railroads in Northern Minnesota around the turn of the century.

Brainerd, Walker and Bemidji were connected by the Brainerd and Northern Minnesota Railroad. It reached Walker in 1896 and was extended to Bemidji in 1897-99. In 1901 it was purchased by the Minnesota and International Railway — with offices in Brainerd.

Park Rapids and Cass Lake were connected by the Park Rapids and Leech Lake Railway in 1899. This line was purchased by the Great Northern in 1907.

Federal Dam, Cass Lake, Bemidji and Plummer were connected in 1909 with an extension (east to west) of the Canadian based Minneapolis, St. Paul and Sault St. Marie Railroad (Soo Line).

The Great Northern also crossed this area from east to west through the village of Cass Lake.

All existing railroads in the area are now a part of the Burlington Northern-Santa Fe system.

A typical logging camp included several long bunk houses, a combination kitchen and dining hall, an office, a supply building, a horse barn or shelter, a blacksmith shop with forge, a shanty where saws were sharpened and a root cellar where food was stored below the frostline.

Loggers had a vocabulary unique to their trade. In the book, "Andrew, Youngest Lumberjack" by this author, the hero, Andrew, learns some dining hall jargon:

Morning came all too early as big Bruce, the head cook, blared into Andrew's ear, "Daylight in the swamp, greenhorn!"

Andrew rolled out of bed, dressed in a daze, then stumbled into the kitchen, dimly lit with kerosene lamps, asking, "What shall I do first?"

"Fill those big coffee pots with water, put 'em on the stove, and when they come to a rolling boil, put six handfuls of coffee, it's over there, into each pot. They'll stop boiling for a few minutes; when they start to boil again, pull them over to a cooler spot on the stove so they won't boil anymore but will stay hot. Then you can bring in some more firewood and stoke the stoves."

"What's for breakfast?" Andrew asked as he worked.

"Stove lids and sausage," came the reply.

"Stove lids?" Andrew asked.

"You'd call them pancakes, " George Wilson explained. "We also call them flapjacks."

By the time Andrew had the coffee cooked and had hauled in more firewood, Bruce and George had stacks of cakes and platters of sausage ready.

"You can ring the bell, Andrew, and then start throwing food on the table," the cook ordered.

Andrew hadn't finished clanging the triangle when the stampede of hungry men started pouring into the dining hall.

After breakfast, the lumberjacks were organized into crews to get equipment ready for the logging operation which was scheduled to start in a few days. After finishing breakfast dishes and re-setting the tables, Andrew helped the cook stamp out doughnuts. Meanwhile, he began asking questions about logging camp vocabulary. "Calling pancakes stove lids kind of threw me," he told Bruce. "What are some other new words I should know?"

Let's see if George and I can help you," Bruce replied, and the two of them came up with quite a few sayings like:

"Coffee is usually called Java or black jack. Strong coffee is lye."

"Milk, when we have it, might be called cow."

"Eggs are often called cackle-berries or hens' fruit."

"If someone wants gravel, that means they want salt.

"Pepper may be called Mexican gravel."

"Sugar is sand."

"They have a lot of different names for beans, like whistle-berries or fire crackers."

"Mulligan means stew."

"If someone asks for Adam's fruit or Eve's fruit, that means apples."

"The general word for food is grub."

"Potatoes are called spuds."

"Sow belly means salt pork and red horse means roast pork."

Bruce concluded, "I'm sure we've missed some, but you'll pick them up by and by."

Logging camps had a culture all their own:
- Conversation during meals was discouraged to help prevent arguments that could lead to fighting.
- Gambling and alcoholic drinks were usually prohibited. In fact, it was not unusual for alcoholics to seek work in logging camps to "dry out."
- No women were allowed in camp.
- No fighting was allowed indoors.
- Sunday was a day off with late breakfasts, games, washing clothes, and naps.
- "Sky Pilots" (itinerant ministers) were welcome in logging camps. Some camps had church services every Sunday, characterized by much singing. T.B. Walker encouraged religious services in his camps.

With this fairly strict atmosphere in camp, the men looked forward to an occasional day off in the nearest town. Here they usually found an abundance of bars and brothels. Walker reportedly had about forty bars during the early logging years.

Most lumberjacks in Minnesota were farmers who moved into the woods at the end of harvest — often bringing a team of horses or oxen with them. There were some professional lumberjacks, however, some of whom learned their trade as far east as the Atlantic states and then moved west as forests were logged off.

The work day was from sun-up to sun-down. Lunch was brought to the men in the woods on special sleds called "swing dingles".

When convenient, logs were dumped into lakes or streams with outlets to the Mississippi. Logs were branded on their ends with the name of the company to facilitate sorting at the mills along the way. On the river drives, the lumberjacks were served by floating restaurants called "wannigans."

More remote forests were served by railroads. Logging trains were usually narrow gauge (their tracks were closer together than long distance railroads). Leech Lake logs went to mills by both water and rail. If the sawmill was close by, the logs were sometimes hauled on sleds in winter, pulled by horses or oxen. T.B. Walker, for example, hauled logs by sled from the northwest end of Leech Lake to his mill in Cass Lake.

The railroad reached the town of Walker (from Brainerd) in 1896. The Leech Lake River was used to transport logs both before and after the coming of the railroad. Once the railroad was in place, sawmills sprang up in the Walker (and Cass Lake) area. Milled lumber was then shipped instead of logs. By 1920, the "glory days" of logging in the Leech Lake area were about over.

Artifacts of turn-of-the-century logging may still be found. There are remnants (though badly deteriorated) of logging camps deep in the forests and earth berms that once supported narrow gauge logging trains may still be seen. Metal detectors will occasionally turn up an axe head or hand-forged logging chain.

The Cuba Hill Tower road (#2133) from Highway 2 into Sucker Bay of Leech Lake was once a narrow gauge railroad.

Logging has been revived in recent years as a major industry, and it is once again contributing to the economy of the Leech Lake area. Gone are the logging camps and the old crosscut saws. Today, logs are hauled by truck and harvested by chainsaws and sophisticated machinery. Lumberjacks are now called "loggers" and they spend their nights in their own homes with their families. Logging is still done mostly during the winter months, starting in late October or early November and lasting until spring.

During the 1930's when the legends of Paul Bunyan were revived, the Leech Lake Indians recalled a legend of their own. They told how their cultural hero — Nanabozho — saved the Leech-Cass Lake area from complete destruction by Paul Bunyan. Just when it seemed white man would not be satisfied until every tree was gone, Nanabozho appeared in response to Pillager prayers. The great Indian took on Paul Bunyan in a battle of giants. Almost as much timber was destroyed where the two fought and wrestled as by the axe. Finally the stalemate was broken when Nanabozho picked up a frozen eelpout and struck Paul a sickening blow "across the chops." Defeated, Paul Bunyan sulked off to Brainerd, where, in ignorance, white man accepted him as a hero before he ruined that area as well.

A narrow gauge logging railroad in the Leech Lake area.

Bunkhouse. Note the clothes drying over the stove.

Logging camp dining hall.

Lunch in the woods, served by a "swing dingle."

Spring comes to a turn-of-the-century logging camp.

Logging railroad, Cuba Hill area. This may be the trail now used as the Sucker Bay road which passes the Cuba Hill forestry tower.

Courtesy of the Minnesota Historical Society

Corduroy logging road. When spring came too early, this was an effective way of transporting logs over swampy areas.

Courtesy of the Cass County Historical Society

Steam hauler pulling loads of logs around the turn of the century.

[1]The ceding of the land by Indian tribes to the U.S. Government made logging possible for the first time.

CHAPTER VIII
Communities
of the Lake

WALKER

The city of Walker celebrated its centennial year in 1996. Compared to cities along either coast of the United States, this is still a young community. Yet, Walker has witnessed several significant and historical events:

- The arrival of the Brainerd and northern Minnesota Railway in 1896, thus opening the wilderness to settlement.
- An enormous white and red pine logging operation, providing lumber with which to build the homes, schools, churches and factories of a growing nation.
- The first significant tourism operation in Northern Minnesota (1896).
- The last major military — Indian armed conflict in the United States in 1898 and
- The establishment of the Ah-Gwah-Ching[1] state tuberculosis sanitarium in 1907 — a healing place for those stricken with a disease often fatal in those days and sometimes of epidemic proportions.

THAT IS A LOT OF HISTORY!

Because the city was named for Thomas B. Walker, a giant in the logging industry, it is easy to assume that he had much to do with its founding. Actually, outside of the fact Walker had a large logging operation in that vicinity, thereby dominating the local economy, he had little to do with the community itself. Patrick McGarry was the true founder and developer of the city and it was his idea to name the new village after the logging magnate in the hope of persuading Walker to build a proposed giant sawmill there. Walker was no doubt flattered by the gesture but as stated earlier he was a devout Methodist and it is said that he was so upset by the large number of bars and brothels in the new community[2] that he decided to create his own town and build a mill there.[3] He chose a site 10 miles to the west and named it for his long time friend and partner, Henry Akeley.

Without a doubt, P.H. McGarry was the most influential citizen of early Walker — and perhaps of all northern Minnesota. Here are some of his accomplishments:

- He purchased the land from Thomas Walker and plotted the townsite.
- He served as the first mayor of Walker (1896).
- McGarry was instrumental in establishing the County of Cass and sat on its first board of commissioners. It is said that he personally named the first county officials.
- He constructed the original Chase hotel, but called it Pameda (not on the lake).
- He was instrumental in building the first hospital (1903).
- He was elected to two terms in the House of Representatives of the Minnesota State Legislature (1908 and 1911).
- McGarry served as a state senator from 1915 to 1921.
- He established the first resort on Leech Lake. Because he started it with 12 tents, it was called "White Tent City," or just "White City". He built a more traditional resort on Second Point in 1901.
- McGarry is credited with persuading the state to build the Ah-Gwah-Ching tuberculosis sanitarium near Walker.
- He was founder of the 10,000 Lakes Association and is credited with originating the slogan "Land of 10,000 Lakes".
- McGarry purchased land and constructed a nine hole golf course in 1922, The expanded course is now called "Tianna".

  Talk about a community leader!

Senator Patrick McGarry, father of Walker

Courtesy of the Cass County Historical Society

McGarry had a close relationship with the Ojibwe of the lake. He made sure they were not cheated by the white men and in return the Indians let no harm come to the whites. McGarry formed such a close relationship with Chief Maji-gabo II that when the Pillager leader died, he willed all he owned to Patrick, including his title and his 15 wives and all of their children! McGarry accepted the responsibility for the huge family. Since he was already married and had a daughter, Edna, he did not take any of the fifteen as a true wife.

At seventy years of age, McGarry married for a second time to a much younger woman, who bore him a son.

In spite of all his financial and political activities, as an old man he found himself heavily in debt and left town with his five year old son and the clothes on his back. He died shortly thereafter in West Hollywood, California, in 1935.

McGarry's daughter, Edna, married a very wealthy man, H.P. Rich and lived on the west coast. McGarry's son, Harrison, became an attorney in California.

The logging era saw several sawmills constructed in and near Walker, including the Brainerd Lumber Co. (the first on the lake), the Red River Lumber Co., (Walker's operation), the Leech Lake Lumber Company and the Northland Pine Company. Although logging still plays a major role in the Walker area economy, it is tourism that now dominates. As we shall see in the final two chapters, there is much for residents and visitors alike to do in this area. The Walker retail district alone has a great deal to offer. Although resorts and lodges may be found on dozens of lakes in the Walker region, it is our Leech Lake that most influences the tourism economy.

Walker has always been the largest community on Leech Lake. Although tourism has helped make the city grow, the community, in return, has provided critical services to tourists and residents of the lake. In the early 1900's, several steamboats docked at Walker. Some were quite large. The Northland Pine Company built a boat about 150 feet long! There was even a mail boat that called on resorts and other residents of the more remote parts of the lake from 1941 to 1977.

As the county seat (Cass County), Walker has always been a focal point for legal activity — everything from trials to property transactions are housed at the court house. This court house, for many years, included the offices of one of the most famous county attorneys in Minnesota history. He was Ed Rogers — a tall, athletic, distinguished looking Ojibwe, who, in his early years, earned his claim to fame as a football player and captain for both Carlisle and for the University of Minnesota. The author is proud to have known him.

Rogers is a member of the National Collegiate Football Hall of Fame, the Indian Sports Hall of Fame and the University of Minnesota M Club Hall of Fame. He was Captain of the University of Minnesota football team in 1903 and it was in that year that he kicked the last field goal in the game with Michigan in which the "Little Brown Jug" became the traditional trophy between the two schools. (Minnesota won the game).

Ed Rogers[1] legal career was equally distinguished. He served as Cass County Attorney for 46 years and was named All-American County Attorney by the National County Attorneys Association in 1962.

As a youngster, Rogers worked in one of Thomas Walker's logging camps. His life spanned the development history of northern Minnesota. Born the son of an Ojibwe mother and a white logger in 1876, twenty years before Walker became a city, he lived until 1971.

Ed Rogers, Captain of the University of Minnesota football team.

The District 113 school system, although based in Walker, serves a far larger area, including Akeley, Onigum and Hackensack.

Because of the confinement of its city limits, the official Walker population is quite small. In reality, however, because of heavily populated adjacent townships and more than 100 regional resorts, Walker's retail district, schools and services in general are more like other Minnesota communities of 10,000 or more.

WHIPHOLT

This little resort town secured its unusual name from two men who started the first post office: George Whipple and Holt (first name unknown). Whipholt is, of course, the combination of the names of the partners. Unfortunately, the two men allegedly absconded with about $800 of postal funds and were replaced by a man named Ray Potter.

Ed Rogers, Cass and All American County Attorney

Courtesy of the Cass County Historical Society

Whipple and Holt were not the first residents. They were preceded by farmers, resorters and a man named Carter who had a store there.

The first white settler reportedly arrived in 1922; his name was Mallen.

ONIGUM

This largely Indian community is steeped in Leech Lake history — most of which is unrecorded, and like most early Native American history, lost forever.

The map on the next page shows Onigum at its height of recorded activity. At the time the map was drawn (1916) the community was the location of the Leech Lake Indian (Chippewa) Agency (first created, however, on the lake just southwest of Agency Bay), a trading post, boarding school, two churches (Catholic and Episcopalian), a clinic, sawmill and more.

Courtesy of the Cass County Historical Society

View of Onigum from the lake.

In 1922, the Chippewa agencies of Minnesota (except for Red Lake) were consolidated at the town of Cass Lake. After losing the agency, Onigum deteriorated fairly rapidly and eventually all of the buildings identified on the map were abandoned.

In August of 1903, there was concern about a possible Indian uprising. The Ojibwe were disgruntled because of timber payment issues and other grievances. The agency people were concerned enough to arrange for a launch as a means of escape, should that become necessary. Chief Flat Mouth II — ever the peacemaker — lined up other Ojibwe leaders (including "Old Bug," focus of the warfare 5 years earlier) to work for peace. Armed conflict was avoided.

Onigum today is once again mostly an Ojibwe settlement.

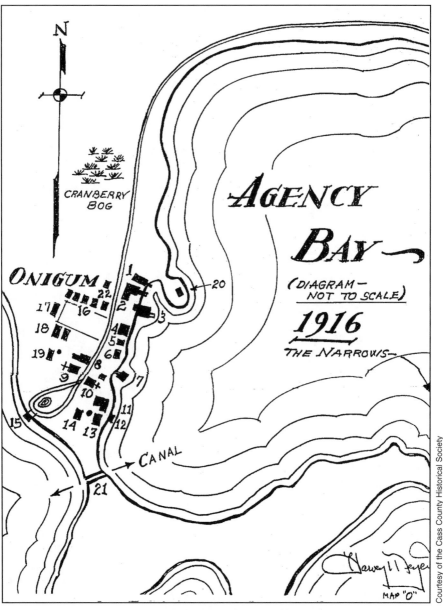

This sketch, not to scale, is intended to show the general arrangement of the Onigum Community between 1916 and 1925. As of 1983 the only buildings left were one employee house, the chief clerk's house, the shell of the Catholic Church, the Episcopal Chapel drastically converted, the ruin of the teacher's house, and most of the original canal blocked by a road fill. It is astonishing how completely the other structures have disappeared.

KEY TO AGENCY BAY DIAGRAM

1. Ice House
2. Saw Mill
3. Covered Agency Dock
4. Superintendent's House
5. Chief Clerk's House
6. Doctor's House and Clinic
7. Public Dock
8. Bilben-Kulander Store (Trading Post)
9. Catholic Church
10. Episcopal Church and Missionary's House
11. Boarding School Main Building — Dormitory, Dining Hall, et cetera
12. Pump House
13. School Building (Four classrooms)
14. Teacher's House
15. Landing on Walker Bay Side
16. Employee Houses (five)
17. Office (of Leech Lake Indian Agency)
18. Commissary and Council Hall
19. Barns, et cetera
20. Small House
21. The Canal to Walker Bay (boats up to 25 feet long)
22. Blacksmith Shop

FEDERAL DAM

Located at the source of the Leech Lake River, which empties into the Mississippi, this is a logical village site.

Construction of the dam itself was started in 1882 and completed two years later. The purpose of the dam was to make Leech Lake a part of the Headwaters Reservoir System, as authorized by congress in 1880. The primary concern was to control water levels on the Mississippi River.

A few whites began moving into the area at that time — mostly farmers and loggers. A home was constructed at the dam-site for the tender and his family. Both the Ojibwe and the white population remained sparse until the coming of the Minneapolis, St. Paul and Sault St. Marie Railroad in 1910. Not only did the "Soo" Line come to Federal Dam, but the location was designated as a "division point," which meant that crews would change here and there would be the construction of a depot, round house,

Courtesy of the Cass County Historical Society

When the muskies went wild – Federal Dam

ONE DAYS FISHING

FEDERAL DAM, M

Courtesy of the Cass County Historical Society

The inscription on the picture tells the story. But how about those white shirts and ties?

repair shops, two section houses, switching yards, and a rooming house for trainmen. The tracks came from Moose Lake (to the east) and continued west through Cass Lake, Bemidji and Plummer. A town was literally born over-night. Homes, churches, a school, stores, a theater and several hotels sprang up.

Federal Dam flourished as a railroad town for several years, but like so many division points, fell victim to technology, diesel engines, faster trains, etc. The railroad abandoned all the facilities it had built; even the depot was sold and moved away.

Logging, another "backbone" of the Leech Lake economy, also diminished greatly after about 1920. Yet, Federal Dam is a community that has refused to die. As logging and railroading faded away, tourism boomed. The community is still rebounding. In 1997, a federal grant provided for modernizing the water and sewer system. No doubt, the best years lie ahead.

The dam for which the community was named has a history of its own. In addition to the spillways, the dam was constructed with a sluice-way for logs, so that they could be floated to the Mississippi and then to sawmill towns on that river. It even has a fishway. Since its construction in 1884, the dam has been remodeled or rebuilt several times. In 1957, the dam actually washed out, lowering the waterlevel of Leech Lake significantly.

For further information on the history of Federal Dam and Gould Township, consult the excellent and comprehensive book by Cecilia McKeig, entitled "Federal Dam."

[1]Today, Ah-Gwah-Ching is a state operated nursing and retirement home.

[2]Some said that Walker was actually embarrassed that the town bore his name.

[3]Walker was so opposed to drinking that the original deeds to the property in Akeley prohibited the presence of alcohol. If liquor were found, the deed was to become void. This was challenged in the courts later and ruled unconstitutional.

CHAPTER IX

Tourism

When Patrick McGarry first arrived at Leech Lake (for the purpose of visiting his brother) he has been reported as saying, "I will go no further. This is the most beautiful place of all."

From the beginning, McGarry saw opportunities for tourism. While others were focused on logging, he recognized the scenic beauty, the excellent fishing and duck and big game hunting as future tourist attractions. He believed the railroad that carried logs and lumber south could bring tourists north.

In the very same year that he plotted the city of Walker (1896), McGarry entered the tourist business. He began with 12 tents, two log cabins and another small building — it was "nick-named" White Tent City. The venture was successful enough to encourage him to build a more traditional resort on Second Point. Although it could be reached by tote road in good weather, it was usually easier in the early days to row the one and one-half miles. In 1901, McGarry added a 3 story log clubhouse with 30 rooms and a dance hall. The next year he added four cottages and enlarged the dining room and changed the name from "Second Point" to "Glengarry." The entrepreneur was not disappointed. Tourists even came from other states and the guest list included governors, senators and politicians — even Thomas Barlow Walker stayed there. Entertainment included moonlight cruises and trips to Bear Island where Native American dancers entertained the guests.

As mentioned earlier, it was also McGarry who built the first hotel in Walker. He called it "The Pameda." It was his for only a short time; he sold it to Bert Chase in 1899. Chase renamed the hotel for himself, calling it "The Chase." In 1922, the Chase family built the present Chase on the Lake.[2] In 1997 the historic hotel was partially destroyed by fire. At this writing efforts are underway to have it restored.

Chris and Marie Peterson were also pioneers in the resort business on Leech Lake. They began by housing tourists in their farm home. Cabins were added in 1920 and the resort was named "Hiawatha Beach." The

Early Leech Lake tourists dressed for the occasion.

The "kitchen crew" at Glengarry on Second Point.

The beginning of a new era: recreation. This well-dressed fishing party apparently used bamboo poles to catch all these walleyes, northerns, bass and suckers in Leech Lake in 1896.

Petersons also had a hand in building Merit Lodge (1921). Since there were no roads, the logs were floated to the site. It was operated by Frank and Ida Merritt[3] and by Ed Kritzan after 1949. Both resorts acquired new owners in 1957. Merit Lodge is now a part of Huddles Resort.

Vera Noble operated Forest View in 1924.

Shady Knolls was built by William McGarry (a nephew of Pat McGarry) in 1928.

Roy Huddle operates the oldest resort on Leech Lake under continuous family ownership. It was opened in 1928 by his father, Les Huddle and Grandfather, Roy senior. They moved there from Richfield.

As stated earlier, Pat McGarry built the first golf course in 1922 (currently the 18 hole Tianna). The facility is one of the busiest in the north country and has been a major tourist attraction.

In 1997-98 a new golf course was constructed north of Walker on the Longbow Road.

Winter sports began drawing tourists to the area prior to World War II. In 1941, the Great Northern Railroad ran the first winter sports train from the Twin Cities to Walker, with about 100 passengers.

In 1930, with McGarry's encouragement, Elizabeth Fish built Camp

Danworthy for Girls between Long and Third Lakes. In 1978, under new ownership (In Fisherman, Inc.) it was renamed "Camp Fish." Fishing was the theme of the camp and youngsters were able to enjoy a camping experience while learning how to be better fishermen. The camp closed in 1991.

In the early years, most tourists arrived by train and most opportunities for enjoying the lake were limited to the immediate Walker area. With the coming of highways and service roads, resorts have sprung up all around the lake. Again it was Patrick McGarry who lobbied successfully for bituminous surfaced roads leading to Walker.

The opening of the Northern Lights Casino at the junction of highways 371 and 200 and the Palace Bingo and Casino west of Cass Lake off Highway 2 by the Leech Lake Ojibwe gave tourism another tremendous boost.

The citizens of the Walker area do much to encourage tourism, including the sponsorship of special events — such as:

- The Eelpout Festival.
- Fishing tournaments.
- Golf tournaments.
- The Moondance Jam.
- Art shows.
- The Leech Lake Regatta.
- The Ethnic Fest and
- Marathon runs.

Thus, tourism continues to thrive and grow around Leech Lake; there is an increase in the numbers of tourists each succeeding year.

It is probably a blessing, however, that expansion of tourist facilities is limited by the fact so much of the shoreline of Leech Lake is national forest, state land, county land or Indian land. Because these lands will probably never be developed, we are likely guaranteed that our beloved Leech Lake will always remain part wilderness, and that is perhaps the greatest tourist attraction of all!

[1]Opheim, Oliver. Much of the information about McGarry was taken from his article in the Centennial issue of the Walker Pilot-Independent.

[2]The original Chase (Pameda) was located in the present town square. The author's great uncle, Gust Kulander, was master of ceremonies at several celebrations and special events at the hotel in its early years.

[3]The Merritt family was from Duluth where they were involved in iron mining. They used this lodge on Leech Lake to entertain business clients and other guests.

CHAPTER X
Things to See and Do Around Leech Lake

OUTDOOR SPORTS

FISHING

Muskies -

Leech is recognized by many (if not most) fishermen as the outstanding Muskie lake in Minnesota. Many muskie enthusiasts who once sought their quarry in Canada, now say they enjoy even better fishing right here. Not only does the lake have an excellent population of this king of freshwater fish, but they are, genetically, a strain of trophy size — true pituitary giants! Thirty pound muskies are not uncommon and forty pounders are caught every year. Leech Lake could contain the next world's record!

Muskie guides, as well as guides for other varieties of fish, are available at Walker and Federal Dam and through resorts at other locations around the lake. Reed's sporting goods store in Walker also arranges for guides. Fishing on your own, however, can be productive. Muskies may be found all over Leech Lake, but for starters, try the weed beds on the portage Bay side of Ottertail Point, the Federal Dam area and the west side of Sucker Bay.

Muskie tournaments are held each year. Some are run out of Walker; others are headquartered at Federal Dam.

Walleyes —

The walleye is the most highly prized fish in Minnesota — not because it is a good fighter, but because of its eating qualities.

Leech Lake is one of the best — if not the best — producers of walleyes in the state. Only Mille Lacs and Lake of the Woods can compare in productivity.

Walleye pike may be found in all parts of the lake, but their habitat changes with the season. In spring and early summer, try shallow water over sandy bottoms (6 to 8 feet) off points and bays. Towards evening and after dark, they will be in even shallower water. During the summer, look for structure (reefs, drop offs and weed beds).

Leech has many weed beds that attract summer walleyes. Fish at depths of 8 to 12 feet along the edges of the beds. In some parts of the lake, cabbage weeds grow far enough apart to allow drifting through without getting hung up all the time; these can be very productive. Although walleyes may be caught any time of day or night, evenings are usually best.

Three limits of Leech Lake walleyes (and a perch) taken through the ice.

During the hottest part of the summer, try the deep holes — 20 feet and deeper.

As fall approaches, walleyes return to their spring habitat.

In winter, try deep water during the day (20 — 30 feet) and shallow water at night (6 to 8 feet). Although you can fish through the ice out in the open or bring your own shelter on cold days, several resorts rent angling houses and provide sleeping accommodations.

Steve Clabots, Chanhassen, MN, with a couple of "near trophies" taken through the ice.

Northern Pike —

Leech Lake contains a heavy concentration of northerns — some huge. The small-

Jerry Hayenga, St. Cloud, MN, speared this beauty in Sucker Bay.

er northerns in this lake tend to be very skinny, but once they reach three or four pounds, they are a beautiful fish.

Spring fishing finds them near the inlets and outlets of rivers and streams (where they have spawned) or they may be in the same areas as walleyes, but perhaps a little closer to shore. Once the weedbeds appear, look for them there .

In winter, spearing northerns can be a blast. Set-up on the edges of weedbeds in 8 to 10 feet of water over a sandy bottom. An occasional whitefish may come by, they are excellent eating and well worth spearing.

Several resorts rent spear houses.

Eric Peterson, Lino Lakes, MN, speared this beauty.

Bass —

Both large and small mouth bass are found in Leech Lake, but not in abundance.

Smallmouths seem to haunt rivers and streams running in and out of the lake, white largemouths may be found in bull rushes or weedbeds.

Crappies —

Crappies grow to be huge in Leech Lake — frequently over two pounds. They are elusive, however, and since they are very much a school fish it is usually "feast or famine."

Early spring will find them in or near the mouths of streams or looking for minnows in very shallow water over dark bottoms.

They are difficult to locate in summer. If you catch one while fishing walleyes, switch to a smaller lure and give that area a try.

Sunfish —

"Sunnies" are found in good numbers and of large size. After ice-out they frequent very shallow water with a dark or muddy bottom. These areas warm up first and attract baitfish. Sunfish spawn in June and will aggressively protect their nests. Try 4 to 12 feet of water.

Perch —

Leech Lake Perch are excellent to eat and grow relatively large, a few over a pound. Unfortunately, at certain times of the year they may be wormy. Small, white cysts appear in the meat of some (not all) fish, each containing a tiny, white worm. Perch are a great "bonus fish" when angling for walleyes but well worth seeking on their own.

In spring or early summer, perch may be found with their walleye cousins off points or in bays. As summer warms up, try deeper weedbeds.

Fishing through the ice for perch has become a popular winter sport, especially after the close of walleye and northern season (mid February). Try deep water (20 to 30 feet) during winter; move to shallower water (6 to 10 feet) towards spring (late February and March).

Rock Bass —

Because rock bass in many lakes are wormy, most fishermen ignore them. Leech Lake "rockies" are different; they are usually parasite free. The meat is snowy white, firm and delicious.

Rock Bass are easily caught late spring through summer. Look for them along the edges of (and in) bull rushes.

Eelpout —

The annual winter Eelpout Festival has given this fish (and Walker) national publicity. They are ugly looking, slimy and hard to clean — but they are excellent eating. The meat is white and very firm. If you cut the fillets into pieces the size and shape of scallops, bread them and then deep-fry them, it is very hard to tell the difference from this popular shell-fish.

After all — the eelpout should be good eating, it is a freshwater cousin of the cod fish, and we make lutefisk from cod!

An occasional eelpout is caught while fishing walleyes, but they like deeper, colder water and tend to be night feeders. They are most easily caught in winter through the ice. Try shallow water (5 to 6 feet) at night along bull rushes.

HUNTING

Deer —

Minnesota's best deer hunting is now found in the agricultural regions, but if you enjoy the wilderness experience, try the Leech Lake area.

Thousands of acres are open to public hunting in the Chippewa National Forest and on county and state lands.

Bear —

Bear hunting has become a more popular sport in recent years and the Leech Lake wilderness areas have as good a population as any part of the state. As with deer, Chippewa National Forest and county and state lands are open to the public.

Jerry Hayenga, St. Cloud, MN, adds his first bear to the deer rack.

Ducks and Geese -

Historically, Leech Lake has been one of the state's major staging area for the migration of diving ducks, including greater and lesser scaup, ring necks (ring bill), golden eyes, redheads and canvasbacks. Enormous rafts of ducks, holding thousands of birds, were once seen annually from late October until freeze-up.

A mess of ducks ready for plucking.

With the current smaller populations of these birds (since the 1970's) and with increased hunting pressure, the rafts have become smaller and more infrequent. But — this can change!

Mallards, teal, woodducks and other "puddle ducks" are raised on Leech Lake. Northern birds of these varieties visit the lake on their

Chad Longbella and Dave Doroff of Staples with the results of a morning grouse hunt.

way south. They are attracted by the many ricebeds. The best hunting — after the first day — is to be found in the remote parts of the lake and on nearby beaver ponds.

Some Canada geese breed in the area, but not in large numbers, nor is Leech Lake on a major flyway for geese. Every fall, however, Leech Lake duck hunters pick up an occasional "bonus" goose.

Grouse —

The vast wilderness area with many stands of aspen make this one of the best partridge hunting locations in the state. There are hundreds of walking trails in the forests surrounding the lake, all of them with the potential for good grouse hunting.

EXPERIENCING THE WILDERNESS

The Chippewa National Forest and the other public lands provide one of the nation's finest opportunities for a wilderness experience.

There are dozens of very good wilderness roads and even more walking trails. The Chippewa National Forest provides (for a small fee) an excellent map of the Leech Lake area. All roads, trails, campsites and boat landings are well marked. The maps are available by writing or calling —

Walker District
Chippewa National Forest
HCR 73, Box 15
Walker, MN 56484
(218) 547-1044

The national forest, state and county lands are open to berry and mushroom picking.

Wildlife watching is a special wilderness opportunity. Chippewa National Forest is home to the highest breeding density of bald eagles in the lower 48 states. There is no better place to see these magnificent birds and their enormous nests.

Other birds of prey, such as hawks and owls, are also present. Osprey are frequently seen on the back bays.

Waterfowl, such as ducks and geese, are common, along with such shore birds as the blue heron. The loon, always a favorite, nests around the lake and their haunting calls may be heard day or night.

Grouse are seen regularly while hiking or even driving the back roads. The song birds of the wilderness are everywhere.

A great variety of wild animals make this area their home. Deer are seen frequently, and bear, occasionally. Moose, however, are rare. Smaller animals tend to be shy, but there is always a chance of seeing (or hearing) timber or brush wolves. Porcupines, raccoons, squirrels, mink, skunks and weasel are common and there are a few fisher and marten.

There is a good chance of seeing muskrats, beaver and otter along the more secluded shorelines.

Experience and enjoy the wilderness!

GREAT DAY TRIPS

The National Forest Service suggests the following:

- SUPERVISOR'S OFFICE (Cass Lake) – This three-story log building was constructed in the 1930s by the Civilian Conservation Corps. Interpretive displays and bookstore. Listed on the National Register of Historic Places.
- ELMWOOD ISLAND (Blackduck) – Located within Island Lake, this undeveloped island contains a stand of upland cedar. Great spot to hike or camp and "get away from it all."
- GILFILLAN AREA (Blackduck) – An undeveloped area with an abundance of orchids and a large, white spruce seed production area.
- LOST FORTY (Blackduck) – Virgin red and white pine left untouched by early loggers. Due to a map error, this area was shown to be underwater. One mile self-guided nature trail travels through the Lost Forty.
- PENNINGTON BOG (Cass Lake) – Containing an abundance of orchids, this bog extends onto State land and is a designated Scientific Natural Area. A permit is required from the Minnesota Department of Natural Resources to visit the bog.
- CUT FOOT SIOUX RANGER STATION (Deer River) – The oldest remaining ranger station in the Eastern Region of the Forest Service. Listed on the National Register of Historic Places. Tours arranged through Cut Foot Sioux Visitor Information Center, Deer River District. Summer interpretive programs are also available.
- EAST LAKE PINES (Marcell) – Mature red pine on the shore of East lake and glacial topography make this an interesting 3/4 mile hike. Access by canoe.
- RABIDEAU CCC CAMP (Blackduck) – Sixteen buildings remain at the former Civilian Conservation Corps camp site, one of the few CCC camps in the U.S. with standing buildings. Interpretive signs and picnic shelter. Listed on the National Register of Historic Places.
- WEBSTER LAKE BOG (Blackduck) – View showy ladyslippers, bog cranberries, sundews and pitcher plants from the boardwalk.
- TEN SECTION AREA (Cass Lake) – This area was protected during the logging years of the 1900s. Towering pines line scenic drives, nature trails, several campgrounds, and picnic areas. Summer interpretive programs at Norway Beach Visitor Information Center.
- GREAT RIVER ROAD (Cass Lake, Deer River) – View the Mississippi River as it traverses the Chippewa National Forest. The Great River is a part of a national transportation route that follows the Mississippi River from Lake Itasca, the headwaters of the Mississippi River, to the Gulf of Mexico.
- MILLER LAKE (Marcell) – This "disappearing lake" was originally impounded by beaver dams. The last beaver dam washed out in the early 1900s. Located along the Suomi Hills trails.
- TROUT LAKE (Marcell) – This semi-pristine, non-motorized area includes 11 lakes and 26 miles of natural shoreline. Great area for mountain biking, canoeing, and backpacking. Hike to the historic Joyce Estate.
- SCENIC DRIVES (Blackduck, Cass Lake, Deer River, Marcell) – The Northwoods Highway, Avenue of Pines, and the Scenic Highway are National Scenic Byways. The Chippewa Adventure, Chippewa Discovery and Cut Foot Sioux Area Auto trails also travel through scenic portions of the Forest.

Festivals and Special Events

The Walker area provides excellent entertainment opportunities for residents and visitors alike. Below is a sample calendar of events spread over a typical year. Check with the Leech Lake Area Chamber of Commerce for specific dates. Their address is Box 1089, Walker, MN 56484 and their telephone numbers are: 218-547-1313 and 800-833-1118.

FEBRUARY
Eelpout Festival
Eelpout Peelout Race (5K)

MARCH
Distributor Show

APRIL
Easter Sunrise Breakfast
Community Church

MAY
Walleye/Northern Opener
Heartland Wheels Car Show
Memorial Day Weekend

JUNE
Muskie/Bass Opener
Church Reunions
Pig Roast/Community Church
Mariner Tournament
Crazy Days
Reed's Classic
Best Ball Golf Tournament

JULY
4th of July Celebration
Fish Fry in the park
Parade
Pie Social/Whistle Stop
Crazy Days

JULY (continued)
Annual Moondance Jam
Leech Lake Art League Show
Ladies Invitational Golf
Tianna Country Club
Muskie/Northern Derby Days

AUGUST
Crazy Days
Indian Golf Tournament
Tianna Country Club
Leech Lake Regatta
Muskie Tournament/Federal Dam
Cajun Festival/Casino

SEPTEMBER
Labor Day Weekend
Annual Muskies Inc. Contest
Annual Ethnic Fest
Deer Bow Hunting Season Opens
Grouse Season Opens
Good Citizens Golf Tourney
Tianna Country Club
Annual Walker/North Country
   Marathon

NOVEMBER
Deer Firearm Season Opens
Festival of Lights

DECEMBER
Christmas events and celebrations
Ice Fishing

Shopping Opportunities

The Walker retail district, along with scores of business places along highways 200 and 371, provides shopping opportunities the equal of communities several times larger.

In addition to the usual super markets and hardware stores, there are several excellent gift shops and book stores.

People interested in the out of doors will enjoy a visit to Reed's Sporting Goods Store — one of the largest in Minnesota. Here you can shop with the sounds of the wilderness in the background — frogs croaking, the cry of the loon, etc. Reed's boasts one of the largest gun displays in the state.

There are a dozen or more excellent restaurants in and around Walker and several resorts have dining rooms.

Casinos

The Leech Lake Band of Ojibwe (the Pillagers) operate two Casinos in the region: Northern Lights at the junction of Highways 200 and 371 and Palace Bingo and Casino 2 miles west of Cass Lake off Highway 2.

Both have 24 hour restaurant service.

Golf

The 18 hole Tianna golf course is considered among the best in northern Minnesota. It was first developed in 1922 by the "Father of Walker," Patrick Henry McGarry. It is located just south of town on Highway 34. Another golf course was opened north of Walker in 1998 on the Longbow Road.

Winter Activities

In winter there are many recreational opportunities, including ice fishing, cross country skiing and a vast network of snowmobile trails.

As you enjoy the beautiful Leech Lake region, be mindful of the area's rich history.

MAY THE BEST BE YET TO COME!